PAPRIKA,
FOIE GRAS,
and RED MUD

Global Research Studies is part of the Framing the Global
project, an initiative of Indiana University Press and the
Indiana University Center for the Study of Global Change,
funded by the Andrew W. Mellon Foundation.

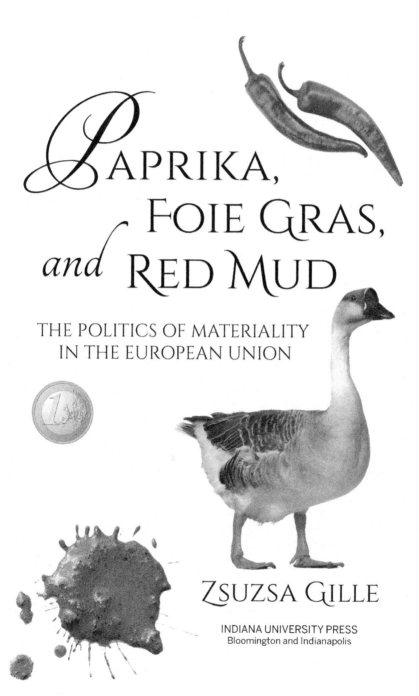

PAPRIKA, FOIE GRAS, and RED MUD

THE POLITICS OF MATERIALITY IN THE EUROPEAN UNION

ZSUZSA GILLE

INDIANA UNIVERSITY PRESS
Bloomington and Indianapolis

This book is a publication of

INDIANA UNIVERSITY PRESS
Office of Scholarly Publishing
Herman B Wells Library 350
1320 East 10th Street
Bloomington, Indiana 47405 USA

iupress.indiana.edu

The paper used in this publication meets
the minimum requirements of the American National Standard for Information
Sciences–Permanence of Paper for Printed
Library Materials, ANSI Z39.48–1992.

Manufactured in the
United States of America

Cataloging information is available
from the Library of Congress

978-0-253-01938-7 (cloth)
978-0-253-01946-2 (paperback)
978-0-253-01950-9 (ebook)

1 2 3 4 5   21 20 19 18 17 16

To my children, Shara and Ábel,
and to the victims of the 2010 red mud disaster.

CONTENTS

ACKNOWLEDGMENTS

I THOUGHT THIS BOOK would be easy to write. I certainly had written about the three case studies and I certainly had an argument, and yet the intricacies of connecting empirical findings to theory demanded that I let this book ferment, as one would a barrel of good wine. Over the years I was sustained in many ways—intellectually, financially, and emotionally—by many people and organizations. Without them the book would not have matured as I now see it has. For intellectual sustenance, inspiration, and constructive comments on the cases and the thesis, I owe the most gratitude to colleagues and mentors: Martha Lampland, Rachel Schurman, Nicky Gregson, Michael Burawoy, Michael Goldman, Saskia Sassen, Elizabeth Dunn, Katherine Verdery, Michael Kennedy, Yuson Jung, Melissa Caldwell, Gyula Kasza, Jacob Klein, Harry West, Neringa Klumbyte, Krisztina Fehérváry, Andrew Szasz, Michael Bell, Peter Jackson, Dace Dzenovska, and the Unit for Criticism collective at the University of Illinois at Urbana-Champaign—especially Lauren Goodlad, Michael Rothberg, and Jesse Ribot. Over the past few years, I benefited greatly from conversations and passionate debates with, as I affectionately refer to them, my "fellow fellows" of the Framing the Global endeavor at Indiana University, Bloomington, especially Rachel Harvey, Hilary Kahn, Michael Mascarenhas, Prakash Kumar, and Faranak Miraftab. I learned the most, however, from exchanges with my former student who has now, in a role reversal, become a mentor of sorts to me: Diana Mincyte. In addition, my arguments gained more precision from constructive criticism by anonymous reviewers at *Eastern European Politics and Societies, Environment and Planning A, Global Society*, and Indiana University Press.

I received generous support for conducting research over the years from the Mellon Foundation through its funding of the Framing the Global project; the Social Science Research Council; the UK's Economic and Social Research Council; the Rachel Carson Center in Munich, Germany; International Research and Exchanges Board; Center for Advanced Studies at Ludwig-Maximilians-Universität in Munich, Germany; the Institute for Sociological Studies at Charles University in Prague, Czech Republic; and the following entities at the University of Illinois: the Social Dimensions of Environmental Policy working group at the Beckman Center, the Research Board's Arnold O. Beckman Award, the Graduate College's Focal Point Fellowship, the Center for Global Studies, the European Union Center, and the Faculty Exchange Program between the University of Illinois at Urbana-Champaign and the Katholieke Universiteit Leuven. My research not only benefited greatly from the conscientious assistance of many of my advisees—Jose Peralta, Taka Ono, Becky Gresh, Grant Shoffstall, and Jeremiah Bohr—but I also learned a lot from them.

I thank the many Hungarians who helped me understand the everyday complexities of food policies—farmers, salespersons, integrators, marketing experts, government officials, and activists. I owe the most gratitude to the many victims of the 2010 red mud disaster from Devecser, Kolontár, and Somlójenő. I especially thank Zsuzsa Halmay, Anita Soós, Mari Márton, and other members of the Vörös-Iszap Károsultakért Kiemelten Közhasznú Egyesület (Union for the Victims of Red Mud Disaster) for opening their homes and hearts at an especially difficult time in their lives. I am grateful to Dr. Ágota Lénárt for introducing me to officials and charity organizations active in the red mud aid programs and for teaching me about the psychological effects of disasters. I am grateful to the Sociological Institute at Charles University in Prague for providing me with space and time to complete the manuscript; the loneliness of the writing was much mitigated by the friendship of colleagues there and by the beauty of the Czech Republic.

My family in Hungary—especially my two aunts and two cousins—have made the hardships of fieldwork bearable by providing me with warmth, understanding, logistical help, humor, lots of home-cooked meals, and sometimes just with plain listening. My husband, Richard S. Esben-shade, not only accompanied me, initially with our children Shara and Ábel, to many of the research sites, but he also helped sustain our home and hearth in two continents, supported me not only emotionally and intellectually, but also by being a ruthless though patient editor of my writing. I thank the whole Esbenshade family for putting up with our crazy travel schedules and providing practical and emotional support.

My friends in Champaign-Urbana have kept up my spirits and self-confidence in more ways and more times than I can count: thank you, Beh-rooz, David W., Faranak, Anghy, Lisa R., Lisa C., Angelina, Manisha, and Dede. I also thank the Hochschilds for graciously opening their homes for a productive writing retreat in the summer of 2013, during which time Faranak offered companionship and motivation. To all of you and others I may have missed: thank you with all my heart.

Paprika,
Foie Gras,
and Red Mud

INTRODUCTION

HUNGARY AND THE EU IN THE POLITICAL AND SCHOLARLY IMAGINATION

This book is about a truly momentous event: the admission of a former socialist country, Hungary, into its one-time nemesis, the European Union, in 2004. By all accounts, unlike most other former members of the Soviet bloc, Hungary—my home country—at the time was expected not only to be admitted first, but also to make a smooth transition into being a productive and full-fledged citizen of this once exclusively Western club. The promising signs were everywhere. Hungary boasted the most open economy at the time state socialism collapsed, in part due to an extensive second economy and household agricultural sector (Lengyel 2012).[1] Its food and electronics industries were already successfully exporting to the West. As a result of political liberalization in the last decade of the regime, as well as the myriad civic initiatives and movements of the 1980s—and allegedly also the historical pride in the uprising of 1956 (Swain 1989)—its citizenry was poised to effortlessly adopt democracy and its related institutions.

Despite such expectations and their apparently high chance of success, ten years after the accession Hungary was a laggard in many common social and economic indicators. In terms of gross domestic product per capita, a common metric of abundance, Hungary's ranking in the world fell from fifty-first place in 2004 to fifty-seventh in 2014. Its poverty rate was higher than during the economic crisis that followed the collapse of the Soviet bloc, and with a poverty rate three times the EU average, it ranked as the second poorest member state.[2] The government of Viktor Orbán, during its five-year reign, rolled back a number of democratic achievements, and the extreme right-wing, if not fascist, party Jobbik enjoys increasing popularity.[3] In 2014, the Organized Crime and Corruption Reporting Project (OCCRP) ranked Hungary's prime minister Viktor Orbán second in their contest for "person of the year," as head of the most corrupt political regime in the world, a runner-up to Russian president Vladimir Putin.[4]

To be sure, if the 2014 elections (national parliamentary, EU parliamentary, and municipal), in which FIDESZ—the ruling right wing party—won by a landslide, are anything to go by, a large part of the electorate doesn't agree that there is anything wrong with their economy or political regime. Could it be that they measure success and failure differently from the pundits and social scientists? Do they make sense of the state of their country not so much through abstract metrics, such as GDP per capita, deprivation rates, or transparency and corruption indexes, but rather through thinking and talking over particular events that seem closer and more tangible? If so, what are these incidents? What stories do ordinary people hear and tell about them? How do such stories affect the interpretation of newer occurrences and thus add to people's repertoire of political narratives?

This book introduces three such events that deeply resonated with people and captured their political imagination. Because each amounted to and was treated as a scandal, each was particularly revealing of a key expectation that was breached. The first such scandal broke out within half a year of the accession: Hungary's signature spice, paprika, was banned from stores and restaurants for several days due to a carcinogenic contamination. The second event was the international boycott of Hungarian foie gras by an Austrian animal rights organization, which claimed that since fattened duck and goose liver result from force-feeding, they are unethical and unhealthy products. The third case is the 2010 red mud spill, Hungary's worst industrial disaster. Seven hundred thousand cubic meters of toxic sludge—red mud—escaped from a reservoir of an alumina factory in the west of Hungary, flooding three villages, killing ten people, injuring hundreds, and rendering the natural environment barren for kilometers.

I chose these events in part because Hungarians talked about them as though they revealed something about the relationship between Hungary and the EU that had previously been hidden. Each object—paprika, foie gras, and red mud—bears an exceptional significance for the country's economy and national history. Paprika is probably the best known in this regard; many people who know nothing else about Hungary can identify paprika as the most essential ingredient of Hungarian cuisine. Foie gras, fattened goose or duck liver, is another traditional Hungarian food, initially tied to a religious holiday in November. Red mud is a byproduct of alumina production. Hungary has few mineral resources, so when bauxite was discovered in the first half of the twentieth century, it was duly treasured as a key ingredient of Hungary's economic modernization. This potential, however, had not been exploited until the Communist Party came into power in 1947, at which point the country became the key source of aluminum for COMECON, the Soviet bloc's economic alliance. As young Hungarian Pioneers—members of the communist children's organization—we were instructed to express our patriotism through our pride in and deep knowledge about Hungarian aluminum; after all, socialism needed metals not only for industrialization and the arms race but also for the material symbolism of the regime's ideology.[5] A key way this economic significance acquired a material presence was the exceptionally high proportion of red mud, the key byproduct of alumina production, among industrial wastes.[6]

One additional fact to keep in mind about these three materials is that their economic and symbolic significance changed after Hungarian state socialism collapsed, and especially after the country joined the European Union. Indeed, they become excellent foils for examining that relationship for lay people and scholars alike. Understanding this liaison has both social and scholarly merit. The social importance resides in the fact that both FIDESZ, the governing party, and Jobbik see the country's association with the EU as one of profound inequality and exploitation, going so far as to call the West a colonizing power. The growing or at least steady popularity of the two right-wing parties would suggest that the Hungarian electorate agrees with this negative view of the West and the EU in particular. My hope is that by better understanding the Hungary-EU relationship we can not only understand why the colonization view resonates so much with people, but we can also provide an alternative understanding of that relationship, one whose expression in political terms is less exclusivist and harder to manipulate for invidious purposes.

The scholarly merit is not entirely unrelated to the social one. To understand Hungary's relationship with the EU is in part to understand what the EU is. Many earlier scholars have sought to provide an apt description of the EU's power, or at least an understanding of its efficacy and deepening integration, by categorizing it as a federation, as a confederation, as a quasi-state formation, as a new kind of nation-state,[7] or even as an empire or a new type of colonizing power. What the analysis of the three stories could in theory provide is what case studies have always delivered: validity tests for theories or a particular case of something universal. But my goal is neither, because each episode provides enough discomfort or exhibits sufficient unruliness to thwart such methodological objectives. In fact, they reveal something that would be, or at least previously has been, difficult to discover in abstract theoretical categorization of the European Union. They illuminate a new modality of power.

PICTURES OF AN ACCESSION

I was first nudged in this direction of inquiry when I noticed a curious contradiction. Take a look at the iconography of the European Union. On the Euro banknotes, what dominates are images of architectural apertures: gates, windows, bridges.[8] The front side of the Euro coins display stylized cartographic images of Europe and in some cases other parts of the globe next to Europe.[9] Above the map of Europe float the twelve stars arranged in a circle—the EU's symbol—creating a halo effect that also expresses an idea of unity: all these once belligerent nations joined under one (starry) sky. The European Union's self-representation shows a strong resemblance to the pictures associated with globalization. Google's image search for the term "globalization" yields a predominance of pictures of the globe itself, with various icons of flows, networks, and brands superimposed on them. Such cartographic images juxtaposed with symbols of connectedness express a certain desire, if not promise, of a particular type of freedom. This is the freedom that results from transcending time and place, mostly the latter: a metaphorical liftoff from the ground,

"Will pig slaughter conform to EU laws? Yes." A poster encouraging Hungarians to vote in favor of Hungary's accession to the European Union in the 2003 referendum.

"Can we keep eating poppy seed dumplings? Yes." A poster encouraging Hungarians to vote in favor of Hungary's accession to the EU.

"Can I open a pastry shop in Vienna? Yes." A poster encouraging
Hungarians to vote in favor of Hungary's accession to the EU.

specifically the gritty, bumpy terrain of localities and nation-states and
the physical constraints of the particular—altogether a freedom from
matter.

Yet when Hungary and Romania were about to join the European
Union—in 2004 and 2007, respectively—the images that accompanied
these momentous events were of a strikingly different type. One set was
presented on the posters encouraging Hungarians to vote affirmatively on
their country's EU accession in the 2003 referendum.

What is the message of these posters? At the very least we can say that
there was an intention of humor or at least levity, as was the case in the
other official pro-EU campaign materials, pamphlets, TV shows, and ads.
The humor in the official materials, however, was interpreted as poking
fun at, if not ridiculing as trivial, certain concerns about EU membership.
Worries about foreign land ownership, labor mobility, or the future of national culture were certainly legitimate and were often raised, but officials
rarely if ever responded to them in public with factual arguments. From
my observations of the campaign and of the debates on various Internet

fora prior to the referendum, it became clear that rational discussion or deliberation was never the intention of elected officials and the experts working on the accession. Nor could this have happened, since the information on which to base arguments was unavailable even to the most engaged citizens. The text of the agreement between Hungary and the EU that contained the conditionalities of the country's membership, several hundred pages of legalese, was not even publicized—if by that one means posted online—until a few days before the referendum.

Another aspect of these posters, however, is more significant: the overwhelming food imagery and concerns about various EU regulations concerning the safety, quality, and ethics of commodities (yes, including that of condoms).[10] This was certainly contradictory to my expectations. The European Union, and before it the European Community, has always argued that its main objectives are to prevent another war in Europe and to promote democracy and human rights. That is, the EU is supposed to be about big and lofty things, not little and mundane ones like sausage or poppy seed dumplings. The benevolent interpretation of the campaign's focus on the latter is that officials were trying to address concerns about the future of Hungarian agriculture head-on, since those were the ones most often voiced by both skeptics and opponents of the accession. But even the question about capital mobility—"Can I open a pastry shop in Vienna?"—used food-related imagery (a slice of pastry), which suggests that the creators of the campaign thought it a winning strategy to associate the EU with appetizing pictures, rather than with symbols of democracy or, in the case of capital mobility, with images of money and wealth. Is this because the Hungarians who needed convincing the most were likely to be more concerned with their bellies than with abstract civilizational values or entrepreneurial opportunities? While this might have characterized some of the campaign architects' thinking, this is only a partial answer. To understand what else might have been at work in the iconography of the referendum campaign, let us look at a second set of images.

Most of these pictures come from images circulated in Hungarian and Romanian cyberspace. Many of them were in a slideshow distributed on the eve of Romania's joining the EU (2007), bearing the title "Europe, here we come." Others are from Hungarian web pages abounding with

(*above and facing*) Images from a slideshow titled
"Europe, here we come" circulated on the web
before Romania's EU accession.

self-deprecating photos of the state of Hungarian society. Many capture the lack of intelligence of their compatriots or just the sheer absurdity of everyday life in a society where people try to muddle through.

While the imagery of the Hungarian EU campaign represents a certain official version of the story of accession and as such is, so to speak, from above, and the second set of images contained in the virtually disseminated slideshow is unofficial and generated from below, they both stand in contrast with the EU's self-representational iconography. These respective figured worlds epitomize a number of opposing values and ideas:

big	small
ideal, ethereal	material
flow, connection	blockages, frictions
gaze from above	gaze from below
opening	closing
unity, order	discrepancy, chaos
magnanimity	small-mindedness, pettiness
juncture, seamlessly sutured	gap

Why do the EU's self-representional images stand in such striking contrast with the Hungarian (and Romanian) representations of the two countries' relationship with the EU? It is certainly not the case that the former set expresses a pro-EU while the latter two an anti-EU stance. This is true as much for the official poster campaign as it is for the slideshow. The latter, after all, pokes fun not at the EU but at an eastern Europe that is still too messy, too stupid, and too poor to become truly European; this is an obvious endorsement of the European project.

It might also be appealing to treat the former as representing something universal and ideal—a kind of model—and the latter as revealing the inevitable messiness of its implementation—a local muddle. This association—of the universal with the ideal, the abstract, and the immaterial, and of the particular with the less-than-ideal, the problematic, the unintended consequence, and the embarrassingly material—is so natural because it is endemic in a particular though hegemonic epistemology. In this perspective a series of binary terms overlap:

macro	micro
global	local
whole	part
abstract	concrete
universal	particular

The implication for social science scholarship is that studying micro-level phenomena, especially in a particular locality, can only yield partial and particular stories, and in order to understand the universal features of, let's say, capitalism or the European Union, we have to conduct research at the macro or global scales.

In that vein the social science scholarship on postsocialism and the Eastern Enlargement of the EU (the term referring to the admission of ten former socialist countries in 2004 and 2007) has either focused on macro- and global-level developments such as treaties, or studied how candidate and later member states measured up with regards to accession criteria and with each other. The more qualitative studies tended to be case studies that were implicitly written off as particular cases of democratization, privatization, and EU accession with the argument that they revealed the bumpiness of the road to capitalism, democracy, and the EU. They were thus inadvertently interpreted as particular and admittedly idiosyncratic variations on a universal theme. While to my knowledge there is no formal social science study of the three cases that make up the empirical backbone of this book, this epistemology would reduce any such case to concrete and unique features of these transformations and, as such, dismiss them as not truly adding anything relevant to the "big picture."

Instead of taking them to be examples of the particular qua local, I read the contradiction between these two sets of images, and their attendant list of binaries, as evidence that what we need is a new reading of the postsocialist transition and EU accession. Two metaphors have been helpful in understanding these processes. Both have been productive but also selective in terms of what type of analysis they made possible. One is the metaphor of tabula rasa, the other is "fuzziness."

Early observers of the postsocialist transition noted that the attendant transformations—democratization, privatization, marketization, Europeanization—did not take place on a tabula rasa.[11] What they meant to convey by invoking the blank slate metaphor is, first, that building a new type of society does not take place in a vacuum, nor can it commence from scratch; people of the future are people of the past, and short of brainwashing them, you will have to build democracy not with the people you want but with the people you have. Not only can one not just purge everything in the course of transition itself, but the local social and cultural conditions will also affect the emerging nature of capitalism and democracy. These arguments were developed and demonstrated in dozens of brilliant studies of land reform, labor relations, and civil society conducted in all the formerly socialist countries.

Perhaps the most paradigmatic concept is Katherine Verdery's (1999, 2004) term "fuzzy property." In analyzing land restitution and privatization in postsocialist Romania, this brilliant and influential anthropologist has shown that private property cannot emerge as a fully formed legal concept that captures reality in unambiguous terms. The practical tasks of what is called privatization often seem insurmountable, and in order to manage day-to-day reality, compromises and temporary solutions have to be made, with the result that property boundaries become blurry and the identities of the owners themselves are also obfuscated. Most social scientists have stopped at documenting the difficulty of imposing markets and democracy, but a few have seen such problems and even chaos as signs of resistance, with the suggestion—more often implicit than explicit—that one cannot prejudge the outcome of postsocialist transitions and that such transitions—especially because they are more imposed than homegrown—will generate new conflicts and inequalities that advisors to the new regimes ignored or promised to be short-lived.

These studies were path-breaking and have not only contributed tremendously to our understanding of this "Great Transformation," but have also laid the foundation of what is now a legitimate and respected interdisciplinary research field, postsocialist studies.[12] Standing on the shoulders of such giants, it is now possible to see a new horizon for this scholarship, one that re-examines and complicates the global-local and universal-particular matrix. Let me explain why this is necessary, starting with the metaphor of the tabula rasa.

The image the concept of a blank slate conjures up is one of painting or writing on a clean, white surface. Certainly the end of state socialism and the subsequent entry into the European Union were radical and swift enough to be compared to "painting over" the old regime, and social scientists studying eastern Europe were correct to question how clean that slate could really be wiped. The previous writing or picture showing through—as if in an Etch A Sketch toy—were primarily seen as obstacles preventing the imposed new writing or painting from appearing clear and legible. They made the new picture *fuzzy*.

This fuzziness, however, does other work besides serving as an impediment. To understand this we may want to reach to another metaphor, one that recognizes that the transition and transformation in postsocialist countries were never intended to replace old with new in a static fashion, but to lift the old and move it in the same direction as the new. The slate image suggests stasis; once it is covered with the new writing or painting it stays so. In contrast, when a country joins the "free world" or the EU it acquires a new direction, a new type of movement, a new mode of change. In fact, movement—in this context most call it progress—is expected and is the stated reason for the change. So a metaphor that implies movement might be more useful for our purposes. I suggest we think of driving a car. In order for a car to be able to move there has to be friction: the asphalt should have a sufficiently rough surface and the tires should have deep enough grooves for movement to occur. Smooth surfaces—think of icy highways—only result in slipperiness, and the car will not be able to move, certainly not in the desired direction. Going back to the slate metaphor, it is not just that you cannot wipe the slate completely clean ever, as postsocialist studies suggested, but that it is not desirable to do so. Some previous writing must show through or some surface friction must remain for "progress" to occur. At the same time, too rough a surface will present greater resistance to movement. The conundrum of EU integration is not whether there should be an attempt to wipe the slate clean—to eliminate everything old—but how much of the previous writing should remain, or, in the new metaphor, how rough the old surface should be for (the right type of) movement to occur.

An example will help illustrate this. In my previous research on industrial waste, I argued that to the extent that the EU's waste policies prioritized reuse and recycling, they could have "latched onto" Hungary's socialist-era waste collection and recycling infrastructure and policies.

Instead, to fulfill other EU accession requirements laid down in the Copenhagen Criteria, such policies and infrastructure were seen as state intervention in the economy and, as such, something that interferes with markets and private property. So all such policies and practices had to go. After more than a decade of a veritable free-for-all for waste generators—whether in industry or households—it was now much more difficult to reintroduce a modicum of material conservation, which now had to be implemented within a ten-to-fifteen-year derogation period after accession. This is one case in which allowing the previous "writing" or "picture" to stay, or—to use my newer metaphor—not polishing down the old surface completely, would have allowed not only a smoother transition to the EU's waste prevention and sustainability policy paradigm, but would have eliminated the damage caused by an interim with neither old nor new regulation. It is in cases such as this that Kristin Ghodsee's (2011) use of another metaphor for the postsocialist transition makes a lot of sense. Quoting her research subjects, she likens the radical transformations in post-1989 Bulgaria to a situation in which one demolishes one's old house before finishing construction on the new one, thus leaving one figuratively, if not literally, homeless.

Indeed, the pictures in the Romanian slideshow in particular demonstrate not so much fuzziness or old pictures showing through, but friction, lack of movement, and dysfunction resulting from incongruity. The same is true for my three cases. The balconies cannot be fully used because of the lamppost poking through their floors (which also creates a safety issue); the newly paved sidewalk cannot be walked on; and the slide ending in the dumpster is not useable as play equipment nor can it fit in the dumpster fully, preventing its functioning both as value and waste.

My use of the metaphor of friction adapts Anna Tsing's (2005) image to a new context. She uses "friction" to show that, far from being a smooth movement of people, money, knowledge, and goods, globalization—like any movement, according to physics—requires a certain resistance of the surfaces and entities brought into contact. Such interactions are productive, not just in the sense that they provide traction for things on the move, but also in the sense that it is from such awkward encounters that culture is generated. Friction is also unpredictable: in one case it may end up providing the much-necessary traction, a surface for something slippery to hold onto; at other times, as Tsing says, it can inspire insurrection, so that the physical concept of resistance manifests in actual social resistance.

Tsing faithfully references the physics of friction, and her research does attend to nature and materiality. Yet her examples of friction are drawn mostly from the realm of culture, knowledge, and identity, and less often from the realm of objects. It is in the spirit of inspiration that I want to adopt and direct this concept back to its original milieu: the material. The case studies in this book demonstrate that the EU is a sociomaterial assemblage, and that when a new member country enters this assemblage, its existing materiality and practices rub against those of the western European countries, whose practices have shaped and constitute the EU. Physics tells us that two further things happen as a result of friction in addition to generating movement—the effect that Tsing pays attention to. In some cases there is a triboelectric effect: an explosion. An example is striking a match. In other cases, over a longer time period, there can be a polishing effect; just think of sanding a piece of wood. Rubbing wood with a piece of sandpaper will ultimately wear down both surfaces—though to a different degree—so that traction and grittiness decrease. This is the opposite of explosion. It is a certain kind of stabilization.

The literature on EU legal harmonization has tended to assume the second effect: stabilization and normalization, a slow, steady, relatively uneventful polishing effect. The paprika panic, the foie gras boycott, and the red mud spill, however, are of the former kind. In them the friction becomes too much, there is an explosion and things come to a halt. In the crater the detonation leaves behind, the pieces may be picked up again, but they will never be reassembled in quite the same way.

When we look at globalization, the postsocialist transition, or EU integration through the lenses of triboelectric effects rather than movement or polishing, different connections will become visible. How to study these cases is what I turn to next.

GLOBAL ETHNOGRAPHY

When we are interested in the question of how something we accept as a universal phenomenon or trend "spreads"—that is, moves across space and transforms places—we are in fact not studying imposition,

or painting over, as the tabula rasa metaphor suggests, nor are we studying the abstract becoming particular the minute it touches the local. We
are studying friction: the process by which things—democracy, animal
rights—gain traction on seemingly alien, inferior, or inhospitable surfaces. This friction, however, is always concrete and particular, because
the grittiness of the surface is dependent on the actual, local context. So
the resulting "contact" itself is concrete, unique, exotic, or idiosyncratic.
What we are studying is not the local particular but the global particular. Going back to the second set of binaries above, we no longer assume
that the concrete can only be studied at the local or micro levels, nor that
the abstract is only evident in studies of the macro or the global. That is,
referencing Doreen Massey (1994), we no longer conflate level of abstraction with social or geographic scale. Massey's critique is directed at David
Harvey and others wedded to classical Marxist epistemology, who tend
to look down on locality studies as inferior in their theory-generating
capacity and in their capacity to support progressive—read universal and
general—political solutions. Let's take the market as an example. Most
Marxists and many social scientists consider it an abstract and macro-
level institution. Massey suggests, however, that if by concrete we mean
the product of many determinations, as most usually do, then the market is not less concrete than certain economic and material practices at
the level of the individual, the household, or the village. Therefore, it is
possible to think of the market as concrete and particular, even as we
recognize that it operates at the macro or even global scales. Economists
and sociologists can certainly distill abstract laws or logics of the market,
but that does not mean (a) that that logic acts alone or is the single cause
of a range of phenomena or (b) that those "abstract" laws do not change
in certain circumstances, under the pressure of concrete actors, human
or nonhuman. Consequently, the market too can be the product of many
determinations.

Disentangling the level of abstraction from social and geographical
scale will yield the epistemological matrix seen in table 0.1.

Studying globalization as frictions therefore requires that I locate myself in the rubric of the global concrete. To understand what this means
methodologically, let's fill in table 0.2 following Michael Burawoy's (1991)
comparison of different social science methodologies. While he never

Table 0.1. Disentangling level of abstraction from social scale

	MICRO/LOCAL	MACRO/GLOBAL
CONCRETE/PARTICULAR		Market
ABSTRACT/UNIVERSAL		

Table 0.2. The relationship between geographical scales and levels of abstraction in different methodological traditions

	MICRO/LOCAL	MACRO/GLOBAL
CONCRETE/PARTICULAR	Sociological and anthropological case studies	Global Ethnography
ABSTRACT/UNIVERSAL	Chicago School Grounded Theory[1]	Classical Marxism Typical globalization studies[2]

Notes:

1. The Chicago School and Grounded Theory in general sought to generate universal social laws by comparing, aggregating, or synthesizing empirical findings from micro-level ethnographic work. The point was to ignore the specificities of the local site in order to discover general societal features and dynamics. See Burawoy's (1991) classification of these schools.
2. Tsing (2000) calls the fallacy of assuming that globalization can only be studied at the global scale globalism.

explicitly identified the methodological perspective he and nine students, including me, elaborated, which we called global ethnography, it is easy to see why I have placed it in the upper right-hand cell. But first let me summarize what that perspective is in the collaborators' own terms.

In the 2000 book *Global Ethnography*, my colleagues and I, under the guidance of Burawoy, demonstrate how and why globalization and its associated processes and institutions should be studied at the local scale. We argue that people in different parts of the world and differently positioned in their respective societies experience globalization in radically different ways (Burawoy et al. 2000). We group these experiences into what we call the three "slices" of globalization: global forces, global connections, and global imaginations. In the first instance, people experience globalization as an external force impinging on the locality and changing their lives in ways over which they have no control, restricting their choices to defensive reactions or adaptations. These changes in general are negative, such as factories closing or welfare being cut as a result of pressures by supranational agencies committed to a neoliberal economic agenda.

People in other positions, however, may find that globalization and transnationalization, or the deterritorialization of the nation-state, also offer opportunities. For them, whether they are migrants finding employment in countries that are better off or political activists maintaining transnational contacts with movements abroad, globalization opens up a space in which they can build connections to improve their lives and better represent their interests. They actively participate in building these links, which in turn sustain them economically, socially, and culturally and which allow them to maneuver around the global forces that otherwise might be more constraining than enabling.

Finally, there are social groups that are not only able to take some control over the processes of globalization that affect their lives, but that actively engage in defining, contesting, and redefining discourses of globalization. They wage their battles much less with a localist and defensive agenda, and rather enter political struggles with alternative views of what globalization should mean and how it could work in their favor. Here the emphasis is on the material power of global imaginations.

This is what this methodological framework does, even as we the researchers are located in particular sites (sometimes more than one): inasmuch as we are interested in hooking up the local to the global, in the above-detailed three ways, we really study the concrete at the level of the global. In my three case studies, I too study the particular contacts and frictions between Hungary and the European Union. After I have analyzed the three events in the following empirical chapters, in the last two chapters I will be able to demonstrate that applying Global Ethnography makes visible a new modality of power in the European Union and will explain why the global particular is the only cell from which what I call the materialization of politics is visible.

1

THE 2004 HUNGARIAN PAPRIKA BAN

Paprika is the key spice used in Hungarian cuisine, and Hungarian paprika is probably the best-known export product of the country. Paprika is essentially dried and finely ground red peppers, whether mild or hot. Because of its unique taste as well as its image as venerable, authentic, and traditional, it has been more expensive than spice peppers from elsewhere. Hungarians use a lot of it. It is in practically every Hungarian dish, such as in the roux of the various *pörkölts*, paprikashes, and goulashes; they sprinkle it on sandwiches, omelettes, and soups. On restaurant tables, the customary salt and pepper shakers are usually accompanied by one full of paprika. There are dozens of processed condiments and aromas, such as paprika oil, tubes of paprika cream, or jars of paprika spreads one can add to stews or soups, or just to decorate cold sandwiches. There is no Hungarian sausage or salami, or really any deli meat, that is produced without paprika. People just don't realize how often and how much they eat of this little spice until they are told they cannot have it. Which is what happened in the fall of 2004 in Budapest, when the government issued a ban on the sale and serving of paprika. I experienced this firsthand. Not only was I greeted by empty grocery store shelves where the paprika-containing products were usually displayed, I also found that all my favorite quick and cheap eateries across the city had crossed out half of their usual menu items because they required paprika, which was now illegal to serve.[1]

On October 27, 2004, the Hungarian government shocked the public by prohibiting the sale of paprika powder and its use in restaurants and by issuing a warning against household use until further notice. The chief Hungarian public health authority, the Állami Népegészségügyi és Tisztiorvosi Szolgálat (ÁNTSZ) (State Public Health and Physicians' Service), found that of the seventy-two paprika-containing commodities regularly sold in Hungary that it had examined, thirteen contained aflatoxin B1, a carcinogenic mycotoxin produced by mold. The concentration was as much as sixteen times the threshold permitted by the European Union (five micrograms/kilogram). While one would have to eat half a kilo per week on a regular basis to be at risk of developing liver cancer, as experts repeatedly pointed out (*Health and Medicine Week* 2004, 433), the state had a legal obligation to act. Therefore, in order to extend the testing to all products containing paprika—which included many more products than the commodities used for flavoring mentioned above, such as various prepared and frozen entrees or potato chips—their sale was banned. The testing and thus the ban lasted three days, during which ÁNTSZ gradually released the list of products found to be safe. Ultimately, forty-eight products tested positive for contamination, some containing as much as 87.8 micrograms of aflatoxin B1 per kilo.[2]

SAFETY AS PRACTICE

Practicing Paprika

Hungary produces annually an average of 8,000 to 10,000 tons of paprika (from six times that much of fresh peppers). In 2003, 5,300 tons were exported; the industry is strongly export-oriented. Germany tends to be the greatest importer, with a 30 percent share of Hungarian paprika exports, while other important buyers are Austria, Holland, Slovakia, and Romania. Hungary accounts for 10 percent of the world's paprika exports. Paprika's economic importance greatly exceeds its quantitative share of Hungary's exports. For a small and relatively resource-poor country, products that enjoy worldwide recognition are a great image booster: the Swiss and Belgians have chocolate, the Dutch have cheese, and Hungary has paprika. This spice is used in many other products Hungary exports, such as Pick salami and Gyulai sausage, which are also important image carriers. As a national symbol, it is an asset in promoting tourism. Not only is paprika production a so-called pull sector, giving boost to other Hungarian exports, its great visibility renders its success and failure consequential for several economic sectors.

Paprika in Hungary has been grown on relatively large farms (the largest about a hundred hectares) since agriculture was collectivized in the early 1960s. Other countries tend to produce peppers on small farms. In Spain, a relatively significant pepper grower, for example, the largest paprika plot is two hectares. Going against the dominant privatization trend after the collapse of state socialism, many of the Hungarian paprika farmers decided to remain in cooperatives rather than return to private cultivation.[3] As we will see, this collective strength proved advantageous as trade was increasingly liberalized during the 1990s and early 2000s. Before the existing regulatory practices and the circumstances of the adulteration are described, however, some background on Hungarian agriculture and the impact on it of EU accession is in order.

Hungarian Agriculture in the European Union

Hungary was under communist rule until 1989, when, along with many other countries in the Soviet bloc, it ended state socialism.[4] Agricultural land that under state socialism was mostly owned by large state farms or cooperatives was privatized—that is, handed back to individual owners.[5] The year 1989 also saw Hungary inserted into new trading networks, mostly opening toward the West, to which the country exported agricultural products and from which it primarily bought high-value-added commodities, such as cars, electronics, and computers. Initially import duties were imposed on Western goods, which made them expensive and thus favored Hungarian products. Hungary, however, soon began to eliminate tariffs imposed on imported goods, and in return the countries to which it exported Hungarian produce also did away with their import duties; this trade liberalization was one of the conditions for joining the European Union. Free trade was beneficial for consumers of Western goods because those now became more affordable, but at the same time producers of Hungarian goods were no longer shielded from foreign competition through import tariffs. This had especially dire consequences for farmers, who had just reasserted their ownership over land, domestic animals, and machinery. Western Europe already had an oversupply of food, to such an extent that it had been paying its farmers to limit their output. The last thing western European farmers needed was cheap competition from eastern Europe, so one of the conditions on which Hungary was allowed to enter the European Union was that Hungary also limit its agricultural output. The key agricultural products for which quotas were implemented were dairy, sugar, beef, and grain.[6] There were no quotas for garden vegetables and fruits. The quotas were determined in such a way that Hungary could not end up with much of a surplus—above its domestic consumption—to export.[7] Meeting such quotas required, for example, that farmers who had previously raised cattle for dairy or meat now had to shift to new produce. This created a hardship, because new investments (in technology, seeds, storage facilities, etc.) could only be made by taking out loans, which were hard to get since the new farmers had no credit history nor much collateral, nor the required business expertise to convince banks of the soundness of their plans. Nevertheless, to the extent that Hungary could still export food to EU markets, it did so at an economic advantage because its labor costs were considerably lower than those of western European farmers.

What reduced this advantage was the imposition of new standards.[8] Some of these standards had to do with quality (such as how knobby carrots could be or how big apples should be), some with environmental safety (such as the type of pesticides used), others with hygiene (such as the requirement that animals could only be slaughtered in rooms that were tiled wall-to-wall), yet others with animal rights (such as that animals had to be sedated before slaughter). Some of these were imposed by the European Union itself, such as the food hygienic standard, HACCP, discussed below, or EC Regulation 2257/94, which required that all bananas sold in the EU be at least 14 cm in length and "free of abnormal curvature." Bananas that were too short or were too bent could only be sold in lower quality categories that fetched lower prices.[9] Others were designed and imposed by corporations, such as food processing and retail chains, or by nongovernmental organizations (NGOs). According to the European Union, as of 2010 a total of 441 food certification schemes operated in various EU member countries (European Commission 2010; Arete–Research & Consulting in Economics n.d.). There are a great variety of such schemes. They can apply to different nodes in the food commodity chain (from farm to retail); they can apply to different types of food (dairy, meat, fresh produce, etc.); they can regulate the relationship between businesses and consumers, or that among various businesses in contracts with each other.[10] There has been an explosion of these schemes in the late 1990s and 2000s; according to a study commissioned by the European Commission, their number increased exponentially between 1990 and 2010 (Arete–Research & Consulting in Economics n.d.). They can define conditions in wide-ranging policy areas: out of the 181 (out of a total of 441 worldwide) actually analyzed by this study, 158 schemes applied to traceability, 124 to safety and hygiene, 98 to origin and specific environment, 84 to organic farming, and 80 to organoleptic qualities. But there are dozens in animal welfare and health, environmental management and sustainable use of resources, and traditional production as well (Arete–Research & Consulting in Economics n.d., 9).[11] In the vast majority of the cases, the conditions prescribed and to be monitored exceed those required by national or EU law, but even when they are at what is called "baseline," retailers and processors can require the certificates, because this is their way of making sure that the relevant government regulation has indeed been implemented or implemented concretely in the way that best suits a particular operator's needs.

What is important to note about these divergent standards is that they all have to do with how humans engage the nonhuman world; they profoundly affect materiality. Changing the materiality of production, storage, and retail, of course, also requires new investments, and these have tended to create new economic uncertainties and dependencies for Hungarian producers.

Two circumstances were supposed to ease such hardships. One was the allocation of the farm subsidies that had been in place in western Europe for decades.[12] As my interviews with farmers and their associations on the eve of Hungary joining the EU in 2004 revealed, applying for and then documenting the use of similar funds, such as pre-accession support for implementing quality and safety standards, requires know-how that they did not have, and as a result most could not take advantage of these subsidies. Another way the European Union has protected domestic producers from competition is the elaborate legal framework by which producers of traditional food and drink, especially those from regions famous for such commodities, can claim an exclusive right to use the name or geographical designation to guarantee the authenticity and alleged highest quality of the product in question. The legal regimes of "protected designations of origin" (PDO) and "protected geographical indications" (PGI) reserve the right to use these quasi-brand-names for products that are certifiably from that particular location or are produced according to strictly defined rules, and embody regional cultural know-how and traditions. This is also the case with the label "Traditional Specialty Guaranteed" (TSG). Parmesan cheese, for example enjoys the EU's PDO label as "Parmigiano-Reggiano"; that is, from the region near Parma and Reggio Emilia, Italy.

Although Hungarian farmers, their associations, and officials in the agricultural ministry wanted to take advantage of these EU-sanctioned certificates and quickly initiated the process of securing such protections for domestic farmers, the circle of products that can receive them is quite limited, so the vast majority of farmers could not claim such exceptions. For example, Hungary received PDO designations for the paprika of Szeged and Kalocsa, for the onions of Makó, for the spicy horseradish of Hajdúság, and for chamomile from the Alföld (Great Plains). It received PGI for a few brands of sausage and salami, but currently has no TSG designations (European Commission n.d.). These legal categories can only apply to regional or local specialties and not national ones, which further restricts the kinds of products and thus the circle of farmers and food processors that can benefit from them.[13]

In short, after accession most Hungarian farmers found themselves facing shrinking markets, increasing regulation via standards, and limited protection from the world market. In this environment, there were only a handful of commodities in which the country could retain or increase its market share. Not surprisingly, such commodities were those that could be claimed to embody Hungarian national tradition and local or regional know-how. This book attends to two such goods: paprika and foie gras. Let me turn to the former now.

Adulteration Practices

Paprika adulteration is probably as old as paprika production. In fact, Hungarians' love for paprika itself was born, if not in sin, then certainly in illegality. After the spice made its way from the New World to Hungarian territory, thanks to the merchants of the Ottoman Empire in the seventeenth century, Hungarians were initially forbidden to grow it; in all likelihood they did so anyway (Halász 1987). Given this transnational origin, it is quite amazing that this spice has insinuated itself so fully into Hungarian cuisine and self-image. While I have not conducted a thorough historical search, the old Szeged Paprika Museum's records show that there had been adulteration in the 1920s and 1930s, and we have little reason to believe that those decades were the only ones when enterprising souls mixed in or passed off some kind of red substance as pure paprika.[14] My search in the socialist-era archives of the various food safety authorities has not turned up any record of adulteration or contamination cases involving paprika. One would expect to find evidence of such instances in the archives, given that many other adulteration or contamination cases, most notably of dairy and meat products, were documented in confidential government documents. Of course, it is possible that such findings were hushed up in return for bribes or preferential treatment, as is the normal course of action in the types of patron-client relations that were endemic to central planning. It is also possible, however, that the absence of records reflects reality. After all, Hungary, a long-time exporter of agricultural products, had relatively strict food safety standards and a highly trained pool of food science experts, which, coupled with the high profile of paprika as an image commodity already under state socialism, could have resulted in stricter monitoring so that adulteration and contamination were indeed successfully prevented.[15]

We have a more reliable record of the postsocialist era. The 1990s witnessed two paprika-related scandals. In the first incident, in 1994, lead oxide was found in paprika being sold mostly at open markets. Dozens of people were hospitalized with various symptoms of lead poisoning, and after finding one-third of the tested samples contaminated, the government banned paprika's use and sale until further notice. Though the tainted product was not found in supermarkets or grocery stores nor did it make its way into exports, such incidents have great significance for public health, since most people—though an ever-decreasing proportion of them—still buy their groceries at farmers' markets, street vendors, or at small mom-and-pop shops. The source of the contamination was a lead-containing paint that sellers mixed in with paprika. In another but smaller scandal around the same time, powdered brick was found in paprika. In both cases the obvious rationale for the adulteration was to make paprika look more colorful, and the culprits were alleged to be foreigners—Ukrainians and Romanians (Perlez 1994). Of course, this framing may just have been a case of defensive patriotism that could not imagine that anything that damages the image of a Hungaricum could possibly come from inside the nation.[16] What is more important to acknowledge in these two cases, however, is that they represent an intentional act, rather than the kind of inadvertent contamination with aflatoxin that occurred ten years later. In the latter case there may have been an intent to mislead customers about the national origin of the spice, but not to taint it.

Many scandals such as these were seen, in the immediate aftermath of the fall of state socialism, as the manifestation of the "Wild East" phenomenon, which, depending on one's political attitude, was chalked up either to liberalization and the collapse of the state or to eastern Europeans' newly liberated and thus excessive and gullible consumerism. But all this was supposed to end with Hungary's accession to EU membership. After all, the EU constantly emphasized that it was not letting eastern European food products, known to lack hygiene and quality, into Europe. News like this abounded in the Western media as the accession grew closer: "A food agency chief has warned that welcoming new members could bring down food standards across the European Union. The chairman of the Food Standards Agency, Sir John Krebs, said consumers could face risks from fraudulent traders and contaminated food unless standards were upheld" (BBC 2003).

In response to such fears, EU officials proclaimed, if not threatened, that "[f]ood safety is an element of the enlargement process where the EU made clear from the beginning that it will not accept a situation that might lead to lower food safety standards or to any risks for consumers. The new

Member states recognize that compliance with the Union's Acquis on food safety is essential" (European Commission 2003, 1).

Well before the fifteen-member EU and the public of the candidate countries formally voted on their membership, Hungary had already not only adopted eighty thousand pages of legislation and case law into its legal framework, but also replaced Hungarian food safety laws with those of the EU, and many Hungarian companies went beyond the minimum requirements by adopting so-called voluntary safety and quality standards.

Hungarian or Safe?

Aflatoxin is a mycotoxin, a harmful substance produced by molds, and as such occurs naturally. Its B and G varieties (B_1, B_2, G_1, G_2) are most common in peanuts, cereals, dried figs, and pistachios, while its M_1 variant tends to accompany dairy products. In peppers, another mycotoxin, ochratoxin A, is actually more common than aflatoxin, but the latter is the only proven carcinogenic mycotoxin (Venâncio and Paterson 2007); many even call it "the most potent naturally occurring carcinogen," which has led to hundreds of deaths in Asia and Africa (Kocsubé et al. 2013, 16).

It is because of its carcinogenicity that the European Union's authorities felt compelled to act in reaction to various aflatoxin discoveries. On several occasions the EU suspended the import of Brazil nuts because they contained aflatoxin in concentrations exceeding the maximum allowed amount, which for nuts and spice peppers is five micrograms per kilogram, according to the European Commission's regulations EC No 466/2001 and 683/2004.[17] While this fungus is thus not unfamiliar on the continent, finding it in a central European product was unexpected, because it requires Mediterranean or tropical climates to establish itself and to survive. Despite ongoing changes in Hungary's weather patterns, such as its increasingly Mediterranean "feel" and its tropics-like torrential rains that many attribute to global climate change, its climate is still not what this particular fungus would have found hospitable.[18] This is how the Hungarian public found out that the famous Szeged and Kalocsa paprika, sold all over the world as a Hungaricum, contained peppers imported from Brazil and Spain. Food safety experts were also dumbfounded that contaminated products could find their way to grocery store shelves undetected, despite the elaborate food safety standards recently adopted to meet EU accession requirements.

The EU prides itself on its image of capitalism with a human face and, in this case, of its agriculture as a reliable source of safe, high-quality, and ethically produced food (Morgan, Marsden, and Murdoch 2006). Policy analysts and most scholars explain the sudden interest of the European Union in community-level (that is, EU-level) food safety regulation primarily as a reaction to various food scandals, of which two BSE (mad cow disease) outbreaks were the most severe. As the EU responded by Europeanizing food safety regulation (Paul 2012; Loeber, Hajer, and Levidow 2011), the food industry responded by designing and requiring ever more stringent safety and quality standards (Codron, Giraud-Héraud, and Soler 2005; Trienekens and Zuurbier 2008; Henson and Reardon 2005; Fulponi 2006; Coe and Hess 2005). Many of the authors writing on this subject also recognize, however, that globalization—to be more precise, the stretching of commodity chains—is just as responsible for this development as the European Union's protection of its consumers and producers, and many even argue that voluntary standards are consistent with neoliberalism. A few also suggest that financialization may also have contributed to the explosion in quality standards. Linda Fulponi argues that the increasing "integration of food firms within world financial markets" (2006, 4), especially the need to be responsive to the stock market, creates an added incentive for implementing and requiring such standards. Overall, raising the EU's and Western multinational corporations' food safety standards has to be seen as not only about wanting to be transparent to consumers and civil society, but also about maintaining and increasing economic power.

To produce food that is safe and hygienic is to produce food through particular practices. Especially according to today's regulations and standards (whether state or voluntary), the way we know food is safe is by knowing how it is produced, rather than who produces it (Busch 2000). Especially in economies based on face-to-face commerce, but also in the case of locally owned grocery stores, the shop owner's or farmer's identity was a guarantee for their products' safety. In the absence of direct relationships and the elimination of the sanctioning effect of personalized commerce, safety increasingly had to be proven with reference to a set of standards. With ever-lengthening commodity chains, these standards in turn have become ever more universal. Today, safety no longer inheres in the quality of edible commodities (such as where they were grown or what species they are) or in the people producing and selling them (which farmer, which shop owner), but rather in a series of sanctioned practices. While we of course may still trust a certain store or brand, the reason a brand has come to be trusted more than other brands—or unbranded generic goods—is because the brand only accrues to products that follow a specified set of operations. In sum, the causality between identity and safety now goes in the opposite direction. Identity, the personal knowledge of producer and retailer, and the inherent quality of the product used to guarantee safety; now the application of safety practices results in (brand) identity.

Similarly, it used to be that Hungarianness—especially being from Szeged or Kalocsa—was a sufficient guarantee of safety; today, however, without the implementation of safety practices such as HACCP (Hodúr, László, and Horváth 2010), Hungarianness can no longer be guaranteed, and the national identity of food products is itself threatened with dissolution. Because non-Hungarian paprika was mixed in with Hungarian paprika but sold as Hungarian, the identity of Hungarianness could no longer guarantee safety. Indeed, the EU's new safety regulations, in force since January 1, 2006, simply reflect this changed reality. Today safety practices are said to be required so traditional cuisine can be preserved. As a recent EU report on traditional cuisine puts it, "A central goal of EU policy is to increase the competitiveness of the traditional food sector through support to improve food safety and quality characteristics that can be translated into greater consumer demand" (European Commission, Directorate-General for Research and Innovation 2007, 6).[19]

This is evident in the case of Hungarian paprika's recently acquired EU protection. The PDO protection requires a precise description of the types of practices that make paprika identifiably from Szeged or Kalocsa. The legislation lists not only particular pepper species (17 for Kalocsa and 20 for Szeged), the settlements where they may be grown (186 for Kalocsa and 119 for Szeged), and the exact physical and chemical attributes of paprika (such as minimum pigment content, maximum moisture content,

particle size, ranges for capsaicin content, and the prohibition of any additives), but also the sequence of actions by which paprika is planted, grown,
harvested, stored, processed, and packaged.[20] This detailed legislation
contains the prescribed meteorological, biological, and physical circumstances for each stage of the production process. Geology is also said to
play a role: the specific type of alluvial soil characteristic of the mid-
Danube-Tisza region, its alkalinity and salinity all seem to contribute
to the unique taste of the spice peppers grown here. Even the fact that
Hungary receives much less sunshine than countries further to the south
(2,000 hours per year in Szeged and 1,500 in Kalocsa, in contrast to the
3,000 hours in Mediterranean countries) is said to create a unique condition whereby even though the peppers may never become as fully pigmented as those in sunnier climates, they retain a higher sugar content
at the time of harvest. "The condensation reaction between part [sic] of
these sugars and the pod's protein content, the caramelisation of the sugar
caused by the drying and grinding process, and the oils in the seeds create
the deep colour that characterises 'Kalocsai fűszerpaprika-őrlemény' and
the sweet and fruity taste reflects harmony of pentatonic tastes (sweet,
sour, salty, bitter, and hot)" (European Commission 2011, 20).

As for human activity and know-how, the post-ripening, drying, and
grinding process receive the most emphasis for both the Kalocsa and Szeged paprika. "Millstones, rolling mills, hammer mills, and mills operating
on the impact principle are suitable for grinding. Grinding requires air
input so that the grinding temperature never exceeds 80°C." Or given in
even more detail for the Szeged PDO:

> Following preliminary chopping, the dried paprika is ground by passing
> it through a tightly set pair of horizontal millstones. The significance
> of grinding by millstones lies in the fact that as the paprika passes through
> the millstones, it warms up. Warming and grinding releases the oil in the
> seeds and the fat-soluble pigments in the skin, which in turn coat the plant
> granules, giving the ground paprika an even colour.
> The final phase of grinding by millstones is the conditioning process,
> in the course of which the moisture content of the ground paprika is
> increased by 1.5–3% through intensive mixing and the addition of potable-
> grade water. Conditioning assumes an important role in developing the vis-
> ual features of the ground paprika, in that the process ensures an optimal

medium—with a water content of 8–11%—for the bioactive components of the ground paprika to exert their protective effect on the natural pigments. (Council Regulation (EC) No 510/2006 'Kalocsai Fűszerpaprika-Őrlemény' EC No: HU-PDO-0005–0393–21.10.20042010, 10)

This seemingly dry and objective description of the human practices that make paprika from Szeged and Kalocsa unique, however, refers to other seemingly tangential aspects of the production process. Several features of these practices pertain not to the aroma, color, or other culinary qualities of the spice, but to its safety. In the quote above, the emphasis on using "potable-grade water" stands out in this regard. Also mentioned are that only whole peppers are used and that the storage facilities are carefully designed to be "pest-free" and to "prevent any deterioration and contamination during storage." The word "gentle" appears repeatedly, not so much to suggest the stewardship or caring by the producers (as we will see in the foie gras case), but to allay fears that the paprika pods may be damaged. This in turn is there to pre-empt both consumers' and experts' suspicions about quality and safety. Consumers may assume that since in the kitchen they are likely to use damaged fruits and vegetables only for cooking, pureeing, or canning—and saving whole and healthy-looking specimens for eating raw—ground paprika may also contain discards. Gentleness is also there to complement the objective descriptions of the manual processes, and thus it implicitly contrasts Hungarian paprika manufacturing with industrial agricultural practices. The same effect is expected of the criterion that neither Szeged nor Kalocsa paprika may contain additives. Of course, machinery may be used in harvesting and drying, and the fact that Hungarian paprika fields are much larger than their counterparts elsewhere in Europe would suggest that not all aspects of industrial agriculture are shunned. More important, however, is what this emphasis on whole peppers and gentleness signals to food safety experts: since mycotoxin contamination—for peppers, most commonly ochratoxin and aflatoxins—is much more likely to occur in damaged produce and produce that is exposed to insects (which spread moisture, creating favorable conditions for fungi to grow), the practice of using exclusively whole peppers and storing them in dry and pest-free conditions is also to ensure safety and hygiene. We see here how the practices of ensuring unique qualities of paprika are blended with practices ensuring safety. Hungarianness (by proxy of Szeged and Kalocsa) thus now must include generic features—such as safety and hygiene—as well.

HACCP is a particularly instructive example of this paradigm of safety, in which safety is no longer ensured by the product's identity, but by the disclosed and branded set of operations by which it is manufactured. HACCP stands for Hazard Analysis Critical Control Point; it is a risk-management tool based on the identification and monitoring of critical points in food production and services where biological, chemical, or physical risks arise.

Originally designed by NASA in the 1960s and adopted first in select U.S. industries in 1973, HACCP is now endorsed by the United Nations, specifically by the Food and Agriculture Organization (FAO) and World Health Organization (WHO). The European Union gradually required its implementation in the production processes of an expanding circle of products, and since 2007 it has become obligatory for all food companies (including the food service industry). Interestingly, at the time of the first wave of Eastern Enlargement, HACCP was not yet mandatory for existing EU members, but it was already required that all former communist countries adopt it into their own national food legislation *prior to* accession. Small food retailers I talked to on the eve of the accession frequently pointed this out to me and called it unjust, and officials themselves warned about the negative economic implications. Hungary's 2007 Rural Development Program for example argued that "[s]ustainability, [and] environmental aspects often put a burden on economically justified developments; or the different interpretation of certain specifications can easily lead to negative consequences (the ultimate costs of implementing the HACCP regulation might as well spoil [meaning: ruin] small shops in the countryside)" (Ministry of Agriculture and Rural Development 2007, 381).

So what is HACCP? Its key novelty in food safety regulation at the time of its first adaptation was that it is a preventive rather than a reactive tool of intervention. It is aimed at preventing contamination, spoiling, or other health hazards in food production and service by identifying and monitoring critical points where biological, chemical, or physical risks arise. Producers and service providers must first identify the source of health risks in their production process, with the help of expert consultants. Then they adopt measures to prevent such risks or to reduce them to an acceptable level. Management entails the adoption of alternatives to such "critical points" and their systematic monitoring. Monitoring is self-administered and must be kept as written records. Authorities in charge of surveillance do not control or test the actual production process or products, they simply "audit the books" to get an immediate (one might say panoptical) glimpse of the state of hygiene and safety in a particular place (Unnevehr and Hirschhorn 2000; Unnevehr 2000).[21]

As is repeatedly pointed out by food safety experts, HACCP in itself does not guarantee safe and hygienic food. Rather, so-called "prerequisites" must be in place before its adoption can even make sense. Prerequisites are the basic technical and infrastructural conditions that facilitate hygiene, such as running water and soap to enable employees to wash hands, or refrigerators to ensure proper temperature for food storage. For non-EU countries, the EU recommends the adoption of "Comprehensive Hygiene Management" that "allows for the establishment of good hygiene and manufacturing practices" without which HACCP would make no sense (Bonne et al. 2005). For example, there is no point in identifying dirt on employees' hands as a critical point for importing hazards if there is no access to soap and running water. So "best practices" require certain material conditions to be in place. In a European Commission–sanctioned training manual, such material conditions extend to the angle at which the floor meets the walls, the color of working surfaces (such as tables) and walls, the resistance of machinery and all tools to rust, tools that are inalterable, and even to color-coded outfits or hats for employees to indicate which zone of operation they belong to (Bonne et al. 2005).

HACCP accreditation is not necessarily a legal condition for the operation of food-related businesses, and there are indeed a few other food safety management tools that have long been implemented in the Hungarian food industry, such as the ISO 9001:2000 and ISO 22000:2005. In order to supply certain retailers or to operate in certain markets, however, they do have to get certified. Certification, like training, is usually provided by consulting firms, and it has to be renewed at certain intervals, even if there has been no change in the production process or materials used. During the period in which Hungary was undergoing the accession procedures and was adopting the EU's case law, the costs of implementing HACCP ranged between 240 and 2,408 Euros per full-time employee, and certification costs ranged between 37 and 1,248 Euros per full-time employee (Gellynck et al. 2004, quoted in Trienekens and Zuurbier 2008, 119). This large variation is mostly due to the differences in the vulnerability of the food commodities in question and in the complexity of the production process, as well as to the original conditions prior to implementation.

It is important to note that HACCP had been adopted by both paprika companies, Szeged and Kalocsa, prior to the discovery of the aflatoxin contamination. In fact, all food businesses had to do so; that was one of the key conditions of EU membership. Why didn't HACCP and all its "prerequisites" prevent the aflatoxin contamination? First, it is important to note that entering the EU was more than a political or economic event. When Hungary joined it also entered a particular sociomaterial assemblage—an assemblage in which paprika, and with it mycotoxins of warmer climates, flowed freely. Second, HACCP exists in a particular matrix of transnational relations and economic linkages. In order to understand this we need to understand safety as not simply a matter of practice but as a matter of transnational social relations.

SAFETY AS TRANSNATIONALITY

Hungary's trade had been gradually liberalized by the time of the actual accession, but some pockets of protectionism stayed in place until May 1, 2004. One was the high import duty levied on paprika. Overnight this was reduced from 44.2 percent to 5 percent, radically increasing the appeal of cheap Latin American imports. There had been two major sources of imports immediately prior to the scandal. Hungary "imported" twenty-two tons from Spain in September 2004. While the same trade event would have been considered an import just a few months earlier, after May 1, 2004—after Hungary's formal accession to EU membership—it no longer counted as an import because Spain and Hungary, as EU members, now shared the same customs borders. This has great significance for food safety, as we will see below. The other source, in this case a "real" exporter, was Brazil, from where Hungary had imported eighty-eight tons since December 2003. Eight tons of this tested positive for aflatoxin B1.[22]

That importing paprika was the decision of paprika processors—rather than of the other food companies using paprika—seems to be well-established.[23] But their rationale for imports is less clear. Some argued it was necessary because the previous year's (2003) harvest was bad due to a drought that had cut output by 60 percent. Another cause mentioned was insufficient color, which was also attributed to natural causes, such as bad weather, though this explanation seems to contradict the previous one.[24] So in order to maintain the appealing color of paprika, processors mixed the Hungarian peppers with those from Spain and Brazil, whose pigment content is almost twice that of Hungarian peppers.

A third argument, however, came not from the processors but from the producers. In interviews with two heads of farms that produce paprika on a large scale, one of whom was the chief of the Paprika Produce Council[25] at the time of the scandal and a member of the Committee on Identifying Paprika Species, one argued that the processors imported paprika from Brazil because it was much cheaper than Hungarian peppers. The other added, nodding, "This processor invited us, producers, for a meeting. He [the representative of the processing firm] put paprika powder made from Brazilian peppers on the table and pointed out how colorful it was." The threat was clear: they either cut their prices or else they would see their contracts lost to the Brazilians. It was also known to producers, and the paprika processors emphasized this, that foreign distributors, selling Hungarian paprika in other EU countries, were already engaged in mixing Hungarian paprika with Latin American ground peppers to lower their costs without necessarily lowering the price. So Hungarian processors just wanted to do what seemed to make good economic sense: keep for themselves the profits that arise from mixing rather than yielding them to their foreign wholesale customers.[26]

Though they had a powerful incentive, and though today food producers everywhere find themselves in an ever-fiercer competition with each other in what is called the "race to the bottom," Hungarian producers did not give in. They claimed taste to be on their side. As they saw it, Brazilian and Spanish peppers could never win against the flavor of paprika from Szeged and Kalocsa. Banding together instead of competing against each other, they refused to lower their prices. After the paprika scandal one could hear news that small pepper producers' would stop selling to the indicted processors and instead they would establish their own process-ing facilities.[27] Ironically, the processors now were desperate to keep the producers on their side, arguing that "we are being hurt together." It is likely that they saw the writing on the wall. The example of Spain, where spice pepper production fell by a third after EU accession due to cheap imports, was looming large in their anxieties. Since then, their fears have proven to be well-founded: in 1996, the annual harvest was 52,000 tons, while in 2004 it was less than half of that, 21,864 tons, with even worse years in 2007 and 2008 (KSH 2013).

Another key aspect of trade liberalization, besides the elimination of import and export duties, is the removal of so-called nontariff trade barri-ers. Advocates of free trade argue that any kind of safety, environmental, or labor standard required by a nation-state can serve as an excuse to exclude certain goods or goods of a certain country from its markets. Op-ponents of free trade, for their part, point out that prohibiting such regu-lation leads to a race to the bottom, in which the country with the least amount of regulation—the worst environmental or labor record—will win. This of course is socially undesirable. The European Union—even before it came to be called that—strove to resolve this contradiction by harmonizing the regulation of wide-ranging economic sectors so that goods could move across member-state borders freely without jeopardiz-ing health and safety. Replacing the many regulatory functions of the nation-state with EU-level ones meant, in the case of paprika, that national authorities delegated surveillance over imported peppers to those ports where these first enter EU customs territory.

More specifically, in the case of the Spanish peppers, since they were not "real" imports—Spain being an EU member—they were no longer checked when they entered Hungary. This ended up being a problem in August 2004, when through random testing—the only kind of test done since EU accession—one of the Hungarian processors found ochratoxin, another mycotoxin produced by molds, in imported spice peppers. In order to avoid a scandal, the processor silently took back the affected prod-ucts from grocery stores. Note that what allowed this discovery was that Hungarians traditionally tested for this liver- and kidney-damaging toxin in paprika, even though the EU had no limits for ochratoxin in peppers and spices. Furthermore, when peppers were imported to Hungary from

Spain, no one could be sure any more whether they were really grown and dried in Spain or whether Spain itself imported them from elsewhere (*Index* 2004).

After accession, even the peppers constituting real imports—that is, arriving directly from a country outside the EU—were removed from the jurisprudence of national authorities, because it was now the authorities at the entry port, in this case Rotterdam, that were in charge of carrying out the prescribed tests. Spice peppers, however, were not on the list of imported goods to be checked. The reason for this is that safety standards are not scientific absolutes, but instead exist in the matrix of economic interests. First, a mantra of food safety experts and policy makers is that there is no absolute safety, there is no way anyone can ever guarantee 100 percent food security. Even if that was theoretically possible, the costs would be prohibitive. Scientists especially make the point that mycotoxins cannot be fully prevented or eliminated. What they do therefore is what scientists making policy recommendations do everywhere: provide scenarios that show what reduction in illness and death would result from what level of mycotoxin contamination (measured in its concentration in a unit amount of food, usually micrograms per kilogram). Then policy makers compare the costs of achieving that level of safety with the costs of treatment and compensation for those injured and the costs resulting from a loss of credibility on the part of the producers, retailers, and governments. It is the already low level of consumer confidence in Europe in particular that regulators (private or public) point to in order to justify the much stricter EU food safety standards than those of the United States or those deemed necessary by the World Trade Organization. But as many experts point out, "tolerable health risks depend on [the] level of economic development and susceptibility of a nation's crops" (Venâncio and Paterson 2007, 40). "It has been estimated that deaths from a standard of 10 or 20 μ [micro-] g kg–1 aflatoxin in the human diet would result in 39 cancer or 41 cancer deaths respectively per year per billion people for a European diet. In Asia a change from 20 to 10 μ g kg–1 would result in 300 fewer deaths" (Venâncio and Paterson 2007, 41). That is, in certain countries—mostly of the Global South—the larger proportion of plants in the diet, and thus the larger proportion of produce susceptible to mycotoxins, means that lowering allowable maximum concentrations of mycotoxins in those countries would actually save more lives. Yet it is exactly in these countries that implementing stricter regulation is beyond the means of most producers.

Second, since paprika production is nowhere near as significant in other EU member countries as it is in Hungary, both in its direct economic contribution and as an image factor, it is unlikely that other governments would find it in their interest to strengthen inspection on spice peppers at EU borders. That the EU seems to be blind to such differences in the member states' sociomaterial assemblages is nicely exemplified by the question it sent to the Hungarian government in the process of the accession negotiations. As Böröcz (2000) describes it, the EU kept asking for production data and information on state subsidies for agricultural commodities that, while highly relevant to the existing members' competition and economic interests, cannot actually grow in Hungary's continental climate. Amazingly, there were questions about cotton and olives. There were no questions about paprika—or, as Böröcz points out, about those fruits and vegetables that had been central to Hungarian agriculture. It may remain forever unknown what the officials who represented Hungary in these negotiations asked the commission about these products—if anything—but it is unlikely they would have had much leverage. Although they were called negotiations, during these talks questions were meant to flow mostly in one direction, since Hungary occupied the role of the supplicant.

Furthermore, the amount of information required on peppers had now decreased. As my informant argued, "before EU accession we tested the peppers for 20 or 30 things; now, however, we don't, because the EU does not prescribe such tests." As the director of the Hungarian Food Safety Bureau (Magyar Élelmiszer Biztonsági Hivatal, or MÉBH) pointed out, the certificates accompanying the import peppers from Latin America "are useless, because they only indicate whether there are any additives in them. Since the EU does not test for mold toxins [in peppers], the certificates obviously don't address them" (HVG 2004, 97). The paprika firms simply assumed that contaminated paprika could not even enter the EU's custom union.[28]

Finally, in pointing out the transnational character of food safety regulation, we must not ignore one interesting fact of the paprika case. Amazingly, it wasn't the application of HACCP to paprika processing that allowed the discovery of the contamination. Instead, it was reported by Slovenian authorities that tested the spice, which came to them via Austria rather than from Hungary directly. Note that it was the authority of a nation-state, rather than the supranational authority that made the discovery.

Did the case lead to any changes in regulation? Three steps were taken in reaction to the paprika scandal of 2004. First, the Hungarian government turned in a proposal to the Food Safety Committee of the European Union to perform aflatoxin tests on import peppers at EU entry ports. The committee turned down the request because it was not convinced that the contamination originated outside the EU (Standing Committee on the Food Chain and Animal Health, Section on Toxicological Safety and Section on General Food Law, Summary Record of the meeting of February 14, 2005, 3). The authority in effect deferred the case to national competence, stating that "[m]ember States [are] recommended to reinforce the controls on the presence of Aflatoxins in paprika and paprika products placed on the market" (Ibid.).

While the European Union–level authorities thus deflected their responsibility for this single incident and for this specific import commodity, it is noteworthy that since about the early 2000s there has been a growing concern in the community about mycotoxins, resulting in Commission Regulation (EC) No. 401/2006, which is not only the principal legislation on mycotoxins in food but is now extended to a greater and regularly updated list of import foods. Despite this growing attention, however, as of 2013, when the last updated list of so-called high-risk import foods was published, there is still no obligatory control at the EU entry points on peppers from Brazil. Only paprika and other capsicum products from India and Turkey have been on the list of imports to be tested for aflatoxin. Hungary therefore continues to have to check for it by itself. Post-2004 records from the database of the Rapid Alert System for Food and Feed (RASFF) demonstrate that while most contaminated food destined for EU member states was tested and rejected at the EU customs border, aflatoxins found in spice peppers had to be detected and rejected by the affected Hungarian companies (Rapid Alert System for Food and Feed [RASFF] n.d.)[29] In 2006 and 2007, for example, every time Hungary detected mycotoxins in import peppers it was found by the "company's own check." These included even cases in which spice peppers from Spain contained aflatoxin and ochratoxin in concentrations above the EU's limits.[30] All other mycotoxins in peppers or paprika had been found "on the market," that is, at EU customs borders.

A second regulatory consequence was that the labeling requirement, according to which manufacturers must indicate the place of origin of a product if it is marketed as being from a specific geographical location, and which had already been in place since the accession, was now more strictly enforced.[31]

Third, the Hungarian prime minister placed the Hungarian Food Safety Bureau (MÉBH) under the supervision of the Ministry of Health, arguing that its previous superordinate ministry, the Ministry of Agriculture and Regional Development, "is dominated more by the interests of the processors" (HVG 2004).[32]

As became obvious all too soon, however, these steps did not go far enough. Even before the police closed the paprika case, a new pepper-related scandal broke out. In February 2005, white peppers from Morocco were found by Hungarian inspectors to contain residues of pesticides banned in the EU. This time, Hungarian authorities went further than they had in the fall of 2004, making explicit critiques of the fact that the EU's standards had been relaxed in the name of free trade (since the contaminated Moroccan peppers were not intercepted by EU customs inspections) and calling for the reinstitution of national inspections. In a TV program, the director of MÉBH dared to make the connection between free markets and failures in food safety. "Since May 1 [2004], all products can come into the country unimpeded; what is more, this is the basic principle of the common market, that is, we should not obstruct this; and this is why there is no obligatory examination [at the national borders]" (Index 2005). What is more, the director of ÁNTSZ pleaded, though still rather timidly, that "[w]e would like to achieve that some control would still be allowed at the internal [intra-EU] borders" (Index 2005, note the conditional phrasing indicated by my italics).

Besides trade liberalization, another key aspect of the global political economy of paprika production is flexibility. Indeed, one of the criteria for EU accession included the candidate countries' ability to withstand the competitive pressures in the unified market. This, given swift changes in consumer demands—and an increasing number of them in niche markets—and in raw material or stock prices, requires great flexibility in production. Paradoxically, it is exactly the demand for standard quality and thus trustworthiness that both the EU's authorities and retail chains emphasize—in this case a consistent level of redness—that compelled Hungarian paprika processors to implement more flexibility in their production. According to various news reports and interviews, some processors started importing peppers in 1997, others not until 2003, in very small quantities to make up for shortcomings in nature, such as the mentioned poor harvest or low pigment content. While such flexibility may be desirable from a neoliberal perspective, it is certainly at odds with EU regulations requiring the listing of ingredients and source countries on the packaging. No processor complied with this labeling law because, as a company president interviewed on TV argued, the composition of the paprika they sell varies more frequently than could be accommodated through printing new packaging (*A Szólás Szabadsága* 2004). Though this may be a poor excuse, it makes some sense.

Clearly the expectation that with EU membership candidate countries' food safety regulation would improve was not fulfilled. This however is not a matter of regulatory negligence, but of deeper structural factors. While member countries are, on the whole, free to enforce standards—whether for food safety or environmental protection—that are stricter than those required by the EU, I know of no new member country that retained standards stricter than the EU's. In Hungary this was certainly the case with the legal definition of fresh milk, with certain emissions standards, or with nature protection laws; in each case the stricter national standard was abandoned. This obviously has a lot to do with these countries' hunger for capital and with their poor bargaining positions. When EU standards are lower—or, as in this case, when the number of contaminants imports are tested for are fewer than under national regulatory surveillance—EU membership in effect amounts to deregulation.

Consequences

The paprika scandal had three key consequences. First, several countries, wanting to take charge of protecting their consumers, reacted to the contamination scandal by no longer accepting the safety tests performed by those Hungarian laboratories that had previously done the testing. Since these laboratories were not accredited according to Western standards, their findings were no longer considered reliable. We see here another consequence of the proliferation of safety and quality standards (Busch 2004), namely the proliferation of standards for the laboratories and of certifying agencies who issue those standards. Of course, paying for accredited lab tests is an added expense for Hungarian exporters. Second, the image of Hungarian paprika has suffered greatly, which has not only cheapened the product but also lowered the value of the two dominant Hungarian paprika processing firms. In the end, one of them, Szegedi Paprika, was no longer able to resist buyout attempts. In 2006, a company (Házi Piros Paprika) whose assets were valued at 51.5 million forints bought Szegedi Paprika, whose assets were 1.2 billion forints, for 800 million forints (MTI 2006). Not only do the assets of these two companies place them in two different leagues, but so do their annual incomes: Házi Piros Paprika earned 1.9 million forints in 2005, while Szegedi Paprika had 4.4 billion forints of revenue (MTI 2006). Therefore, industry representatives I interviewed might be correct when they say that Házi Piros Paprika is only a proxy buyer, and, furthermore, they claim to know that it has made the purchase on behalf of a large foreign food-retailing corporation. In addition to this buyout, and the precipitous decline in paprika production, the other major firm in the industry, Kalocsai Fűszerpaprika, also continued to operate with a deficit. While the industry's decline cannot directly and exclusively be attributed to the ban of 2004, processors' increasing substitution of cheap import paprika for Hungarian makes more sense when the former no longer enjoys the respect and added value it once had.

CAN A FUNGUS SPEAK?

With a tongue-in-cheek reference to Gayatri Spivak's (1988) and then Timothy Mitchell's (2002) questions—"can the subaltern speak?" and "can a mosquito speak?" respectively—what would a fungus say if asked about this case? What do its presence and the havoc it brought reveal about the materiality and the power of the European Union? Here is my ventriloquist summary: The insertion of Hungary into EU networks of commerce and safety monitoring made rational new modes of paprika production and opened up new channels by which a fungus could enter the country. This entry resulted in a contamination that led to the exclusion of Hungarian paprika exports from exactly those western European markets whose accessibility was the rationale for opening up Hungarian markets and eliminating national-level scrutiny for various contaminants. Rather than exporting them, the country now imported more and more spice peppers. Trade liberalization and the relaxation of national food safety standards contributed to the cheapening of the image of paprika from Szeged and Kalocsa and increased the rationale for substituting their products with cheap imports. The industry experienced a major decline.

The expectation that Hungary could just keep producing the same product for a wider economic market proved naïve, however, not only because of the underestimation of competitive pressures and the miscalculation of the gains to be made from trade liberalization, but also because of the assumption that the market is a purely social institution. On the contrary: the market is made up of practices that determine which actors can access it under what conditions. By the time Hungary joined the EU, western European food producers and retailers had enjoyed decades of CAP subsidies, accumulated the know-how of producing, processing, and marketing food for the discerning European consumer, and had shaped the food safety regulations Hungary had to adopt. Another way of saying this is that they had managed to upscale their practices to the supranational—EU—level, so that what previously may have been a micro- or national-level practice now had the force of a global institution behind it. This sociomaterial assemblage was quite different from Hungary's, and this friction led to the "triboelectric effect," a term a cookbook humorously used to refer to the Great Paprika Crisis of 2004 (Sasvari 2005). The friction in part resulted from the fact that paprika was uniquely important to Hungary—but not to the core members of the EU—which justified the strict testing and the hefty import duty on imports before 2004. The fact that after the scandal the Hungarian government failed to resolve the friction by changing EU-level regulatory practices—that Hungary could not upscale its own food safety practices—indicates that in the long run the polishing effect of the friction has prevailed. The edges of Hungary's unruly sociomaterial assemblage have been smoothed out: paprika not protected by PDO certification may now be redder, due to the mixing in of highly pigmented imports, and it may now even be safer, but as a commodity it is no longer as important, it is no longer as respected, and, frankly, it is less and less Hungarian.

2

ex©

THE 2008 FOIE GRAS
BOYCOTT

THE ANTI-FOIE GRAS CAMPAIGN

I n the summer of 2008 an Austrian animal rights organization declared a boycott of Hungarian foie gras (fattened goose or duck
liver). The product requires the force-feeding of the birds and thus allegedly constitutes animal torture. Foie gras, which in French means fattened goose or duck liver, is not exclusive to French cuisine. Fattened
goose liver is also a traditional Hungarian dish that was originally prepared and served on the feast day of Saint Márton in November. Today
Hungarians consume it with some regularity; 83 percent of the respondents in a 2009 survey reported liking it (Élelmiszeripari Gazdaságtan
Tanszék 2009).

The unique and highly coveted taste of fattened duck or goose liver
results from the force-feeding of the birds, which the French call gavage.
This practice enlarges and intensifies the flavor of the bird's livers. Geese
and ducks possess a natural tendency to overeat in preparation for their
fall migration (Greenberg and Marra 2005; Youatt 2011), which is why
foie gras was originally a seasonal product. With gavage this seasonality
is escaped.

Starting in the 1980s, animal rights activists began targeting foie gras
production as inhumane, and the campaign grew wider and louder in the
early 2000s. Activists raised four specific objections. First is the culling
of male ducklings because their livers cannot be fattened. The second

issue concerns the conditions within the barns, more specifically the metal bars on the floors of the cages that can injure the birds' legs. The most criticized aspect of the process is force-feeding. Anti–foie gras activists argue that force-feeding causes pain, gagging, and injuries to the birds' esophagi, and that their enlarged liver is a symptom of a disease that causes suffering and "untimely death." Finally, they argue that the slaughtering technology is itself inhumane, because the birds are not always unconscious by the time they reach the slaughtering station.

The campaign has been remarkably successful, mostly because of the star quality of its spokespersons. The anti–foie gras campaign has enjoyed the support of such diverse figures as Pope John Paul II, liberal NGOs, the City Council of Chicago, the actor and politician Arnold Schwarzenegger, the former James Bond portrayer Roger Moore, and the Dutch and British royalty—demonstrating the relative independence of such ethical projects from political and cultural identity. Today there is a ban on foie gras production in fourteen European countries and Israel. Among these countries, only Israel had significant foie gras production before the ban (three hundred tons). Israel ceased production in 2003, in part to make sure kosher principles were not violated, and subsequently several Israeli producers moved their operations to Hungary (Caro 2009). France, the biggest foie gras producer and consumer, however, not only refused to implement such a ban, but in 2006 even passed legislation that declared foie gras a part of French cultural heritage, thus in need of protection. What's more, in 2010 UNESCO added "the gastronomic meal of the French" to the world's "intangible cultural heritage" (DeSoucey 2010; UNESCO n.d.).

The European Union's official stance on the ethics of gavage is vague. While the Scientific Committee on Animal Health and Welfare recommends that force-feeding be eventually phased out because it "is detrimental to the welfare of the birds" (SCAHAW 1998), there is no clear mechanism by which this scientific recommendation will lead to an executable change in policy. The Hungarian experts and scholars I interviewed all expressed doubt that the EU would ban foie gras in the foreseeable future, precisely because France is such a potent member of this supranational organization. The anti–foie gras campaign, while successful in individual EU-member countries, demands the implementation of stricter standards than what the EU currently has on its books (Földvári 2009). This movement therefore hopes to achieve a global ban on foie gras production not from above, by changing supranational organizations' regulation, but rather from below, through member states' individual reactions to popular pressure.

The campaign arrived to Hungary in the summer of 2008, wreaking major havoc on the Hungarian poultry industry. The Austrian animal rights group Vier Pfoten (Four Paws, or FP) compiled a blacklist of Hungarian companies involved in fattened poultry products and simultaneously embarked on a media campaign, primarily in Germany and Austria, where most Hungarian poultry is exported.[1] The target of the campaign was ultimately consumers in Germany and Austria, who ideally were to put pressure on Hungarian producers, primarily on the biggest producer, Hungerit, by withholding their purchasing power. The campaign was successful in that nine supermarket chains in those two countries stopped selling not only Hungarian foie gras, but *all* Hungarian poultry products. The Hungarian poultry sector reported a shortfall of 4–4.5 billion forints (about US$19 million) that resulted from the lost exports.

The response to this campaign—from farmers, from Hungerit, from the government, and from Hungarian consumers and citizens in general—has been unequivocally negative. Even a major Hungarian animal rights organization eventually condemned it. A look at the economic interests involved helps to understand the key sources of disagreement better.

THE POLITICAL ECONOMY OF GAVAGE

At the time of the boycott in 2008, Hungary was the second largest producer of duck and goose liver (2,000 tons annually) after France, which produced an annual 16,000 tons, out of a world total of around 20,000 tons. Bulgaria's production has been growing faster, and in 2009 it was projected to become the second largest producer with 2,200 tons. Since the French consume almost all their own goose and duck liver, Hungary was the largest exporter of foie gras at the time. In contrast to the French, who export a diverse pool of luxury pâté products, Hungarians tend to export goose liver unprocessed. China has been steadily increasing its output as well. Its foie gras production was projected to reach an annual

1,000 tons by 2011, and in 2012 it opened the world's largest goose farm and foie gras factory in Jiangxi Province, funded by a U.S. investor.

The entire commodity chain of foie gras production in Hungary, from hatching through the initial raising of the geese to their subsequent fattening and slaughter, is coordinated by so-called integrators. These people, themselves experienced in goose raising, are in charge of distributing the eggs or birds and administering contracts with the slaughterhouses. The integrators are also engaged in assisting farmers with new regulations and getting information out about feed, prices, etc. After two to three weeks of fattening (the period of using gavage), the birds are slaughtered. This can take place at the facilities of the meat processing company, such as Hungerit, or the farmers can rent a certified slaughterhouse and do it themselves. According to one integrator, who is herself also a goose farmer, the maximum annual number of fattening cycles on a single farm is eighteen, and many farmers perform fewer. She explained that no family farm can handle more than three thousand geese a year; beyond that volume they would need to hire extra help, and the costs of employees are prohibitive. Thus there is a built-in limit on the size of goose farms. Goose fattening also has a certain rhythm: there are intense periods of work, after which one gets paid a relatively large sum, and then periods between cycles, when income is meager, or at least dependent on whatever other economic activity takes place on the farm. Integrators are encouraging farmers to decrease the number of cycles to decrease overproduction. Currently in Hungary there is demand for only about 2.5 million geese (for both foie gras and meat), which is a million fewer than what are produced annually. To keep the market from overproducing, integrators try to convince farmers to extend the downtime between cycles of fattening. This means that income is far from predictable or steady.

As for income levels, farmers' largest expense is the birds themselves, followed by feed, and then by electricity, water, and other utility-type expenses, occasional medication (such as antibiotics), and various administrative and transportation costs.[2] In the early 2000s the profit rate earned in geese fattening declined, mostly due to the rise in feed prices outstripping the growth in price of fattened geese products. The integrator said that when she herself was only a goose farmer, in her worst month she made only 50,000 forints (US$217 at 2009 exchange rates), which was below the poverty level. This figure of course is not indicative of actual overall earnings and depends on the price of feed, on how much of the feed is produced on the same farm that raises the geese, and on the size of the farm. The relative uncertainty and cyclicality of income, however, means that any unexpected event, such as an epidemic, a grocery chain introducing new standards (of quality, hygiene, or animal welfare), or a boycott can push the smaller farmers to the brink. What has reduced this uncertainty in the most recent past is the operation of integrators, who provide a contract for a fixed amount at fixed prices. These middlemen, however, just as in other parts of the food and agricultural sector, tend also to be the providers of the necessary input materials and are the obligatory entry points to the food processing companies, and as such their presence can create a relationship of dependency for farmers.

Hungerit is the biggest foie gras producer in Hungary. Although fattened poultry products are not the main source of profit for Hungerit, they yield a higher profit margin than other meat products. In addition, Hungerit's fame for this high-quality food commodity is transferred to its other products, which thus gain a certain "value-added."[3] Hungerit was one of the companies specifically named on Four Paws' blacklist, and the boycott exerted the most severe impact on this company. In addition to its size and share of the market, it is also an important economic actor in the poultry industry because it owns what is said to be the country's most high-tech poultry processing plant. Its state-of-the-art meat processing factory in Szentes had been rebuilt—partly with EU funds—and the slaughtering practice meets strict EU standards: the birds are stunned unconscious before slaughter, and the space where this happens is suffused with blue light, which is said to calm the birds. Another aspect of its importance is that Hungerit is the second biggest employer in Csongrád County. As a high-ranking officer of the firm claimed, if the firm did not survive, the workers would have no other employment options, due both to their low level of education and to the absence of other employers in the region.

Hungerit's main Hungarian competitor is Hunent, a supplier of the German firm Wiesenhof, the world's largest processor of waterfowl. Wiesenhof is part of a corporate conglomerate that is not only the largest poultry processor in Germany but also operates that country's largest supermarket chain. At the same time, it has a much smaller share of fattened poultry production in Hungary than Hungerit. It is for this reason that Wiesenhof had tried to buy Hungerit a few months before FP's campaign. The buyout attempt proved unsuccessful, and the fact that Pannon Lúd, a foie gras–producing subsidiary of Hunent, was missing from the first version of the blacklist gave rise to suspicions that FP was acting on behalf of this competitor and was perhaps even funded by it. FP representatives never explicitly denied this, and indeed such claims are difficult to prove, though the fact that several courts in various jurisdictions and various cases have found that the suits brought against Four Paws in the recent years have merit indicates that there is at least circumstantial evidence in favor of this suspicion.[4] It is also a fact that by crippling a key product line of Hungerit, Wiesenhof would exert significant control over the entire Hungarian poultry market. Hungerit and the Hungarian Poultry Product Committee suspect that this unsuccessful buyout attempt of the country's most high-tech processing plant was behind Four Paws' campaign. Most respondents to the aforementioned 2009 survey also believed economic interests to be behind the anti–foie gras campaign. To summarize, there are strong reasons, if not sufficient evidence, to suggest that the boycott was economically advantageous to certain western European meat producers.

ETHICS AS TRANSNATIONALITY

As is clear from this description of the case, the impetus for the boycott came from abroad and received little sympathy from Hungarians, including some Hungarian animal rights activists. The way Four Paws presented Hungarian foie gras production to the Austrian and German public was to contrast a presence of ethics on their part with the absence of ethics on the part of the Hungarian poultry industry and of the Hungarian Agricultural Ministry, rather than presenting it as a case of differing ethics. It is the latter position that social constructivism subscribes to, but political mobilization around ethical issues, whether involving animals, humans, or the environment, tends to rely on the ethical/unethical binary. A matter of difference is turned into a matter of ranking, so that Hungary's ethical norms do not simply diverge from most Western countries', but are inferior to them.

The choice social scientists face, however, does not consist of either taking a side or embracing moral relativism—the position that since there are only differences and no objectively definable hierarchies of different ethical positions, anything goes. Political theory, informed by Habermasian approaches, defines two tests to determine an NGO's legitimacy: a substantive test and a procedural test. The former measures how closely the NGO's principles are shared by the community or culture in which it operates, while the latter asks whether it operates in a way that fulfills its substantive principles (Vedder 2007). The substantive test has serious shortcomings, because it inevitably renders progressive causes for the protection of certain minorities morally illegitimate. This is summarized in the claim of U.S. civil rights activists that decisions concerning a minority, such as gays or ethnic and religious minorities, should never be left up to the majority and thus should not be decided by elections and referenda. Despite its conservative bias, however, the substantive test can be a useful analytical tool when the goal is to understand the rationale that informs an organization's political rhetoric. NGOs always have to take into account how the values they reference in a campaign will be seen by their peers and by society as a whole. It is useful to think of substantive and procedural testing as something NGOs subject themselves to in their considerations about campaign rhetoric. We will now see how the expected low scoring on especially the substantive tests forced FP to Hungarianize its moral discourse, and what effect this had.

A key aspect of the substantive test in this case is how not just German and Austrian consumers, but also Hungarian producers and consumers, view gavage. A survey conducted in the aftermath of the boycott (Élelmiszeripari Gazdaságtan Tanszék 2009) found that most people do not think force-feeding causes pain, nor do they think in any case that animals' well-being is more important than the livelihood of people working in the poultry sector or the preservation of Hungarian cultural heritage.[5] Most respondents (close to half) also said that Hungary should not give in in the event of an EU ban on foie gras production, since this is "a Hungarian internal affair."

Another aspect of the substantive criterion of legitimacy is whether FP's campaign is actually consistent with its goals to help animals. This is where science can be invoked. The science of animal welfare is no different from other policy applications of science. As with most issues, there is some disagreement, and often such disagreements reflect divergent interests. France's official scientific position is that gavage is not torture. The Hungarian Chamber of Veterinarians (HCV) tested the effects of force-feeding on goose physiology and behavior (Élelmiszeripari Gazdaságtan Tanszék 2009), and on the basis of these tests similarly argued that if done professionally, force-feeding causes neither pain, nor fear, nor irreversible pathological changes in geese. The head of the HCV told me they did this study on their own initiative and at their own expense, out of a sense of professional obligation.

What else did this study find? First, the official statement emphasizes that geese have a natural tendency to significantly elevate their food intake prior to their migration; thus, temporarily increasing the size of their portions is not inimical to their biology. This means that birds do not become sick and that the meat they produce is not unhealthy for consumption, as Four Paws alleged. Second, the report rejects the comparison that animal rights activists draw between force-feeding humans and geese, as they do in their anti–foie gras street theater, in which an activist is pinned to her seat by a huge tube in her mouth, which is connected to a big funnel. The veterinarians argued that geese's esophagi have no feeling in them. Unlike humans, they do not gag or feel pain when the tube is inserted in their mouths. They may simply feel increased pressure from the feeding tubes. While this official report convinced the main Hungarian animal rights organization, Fehérkereszt (White Cross), that gavage is not torture, Four Paws accused the HCV of bowing to the interests of the poultry lobby. It was at this point that Fehérkereszt and Four Paws parted ways.

HCV emphasized that this does not mean that there are no better or worse practices of gavage; in fact, HCV is involved in educating farmers about how to increase the birds' comfort. An example of this is their advocacy of using rubber tubes for feeding, which due to their flexibility reduces the discomfort birds might feel during force-feeding. They have also endorsed and encouraged the mechanization of feeding, because the traditional manual feeding method is more likely to lead to overfeeding and to the feed getting into the breathing passages of the birds. The traditional method consists of shoving a handful of corn meal in the beaks of geese and then squeezing the lump of feed down the esophagi of the birds. (This is a practice I observed in the countryside as a child.) That is, HCV does not argue that the birds feel no discomfort, simply that this does not lead to disease, and that this discomfort is not pain. It is exactly in this semiotic difference between pain and discomfort that one can see that this particular ethical question cannot be answered by science alone. Furthermore, it is this inherent subjectivity of scientific evaluations that necessitates both other scientific interventions and the shift of the debate onto the terrain of culture and national tradition.

The other aspect of scientific arguments concerns the comparison of different types of animal suffering. Here laypeople's own rationality is also a kind of scientific exercise and thus deserves some attention. The farmers and integrators interviewed brought up a number of such comparisons. One commonly mentioned was broiler chickens that live a shorter and much crueler life than geese and never see sunlight. Compared to them, geese are relatively free to roam around. Their argument did not rest mainly on the contrast between the chickens' and geese's quality of life, but on the sheer size of the chicken sector. Fehérkereszt also argued that if Four Paws really wanted to make an impact, it would focus not on geese and ducks that constitute such a small segment of meat production, but on industrial chicken farms and on the conditions of live fish for sale. Another comparison was boiling lobsters alive. The significance of this comparison was not the relative size of lobster consumption, as with chickens and fish; quite the contrary. Hungarians rarely eat lobster, and most will likely never taste it. It is, however, an iconic Western luxury food. By making frequent references to lobsters, they were emphasizing how the allegedly civilized West engages in even more barbaric treatment of animals than gavage. Finally, as one integrator told me, "A goose will surely not put itself on the feeding tube, but neither will a horse harness itself to a carriage nor be pleased to be saddled." This time the comparison is to a practice familiar to Hungarians and others. By creating an analogy between gavage and a taken-for-granted and universal practices, the logic of the anti–foie gras campaign itself can be called into question, suggesting that if these same activists wanted to be consistent they would have to oppose the riding and use in transport of horses as well.

Science, in theory, could measure the discomfort or pain of animals in all these cases, and animal rights activists could then use such results to rank the importance of their causes. But science is never invoked to justify the selection of a cause, only to justify the claims for eliminating torture once the cause is selected. After all, as many of my research subjects suggested, if science played a role in selecting causes, let's say by focusing on the largest sector of meat production or the most amount of suffering, animal activists would likely focus their efforts on broiler chickens or lobsters, respectively. This brief overview of the use of science in the debate suggests that expertise can never be the only arbiter in ethical food conflicts. This is exactly why FP had to argue that birds were not only tortured but were diseased as well, reframing the campaign as one of food safety rather than ethics.

Another aspect of the substantive test is the ranking of ethical concerns in the society in which the NGO operates. Right after the Four Paws campaign began, Hungerit stopped its production of foie gras and laid off employees who worked on that production line. In response, workers themselves staged a street demonstration in front of the Budapest office of FP. They carried signs with messages such as "Look us in the eye!," implying that the organization had failed to engage them in a dialogue, or "Protect humans, not just animals!," expressing a feeling that they are discounted as humans. Similarly, one employee of Hungerit threatened with unemployment asked, "Is it not human torture that we will be kicked out onto the street?" In addition to protesting against the campaign on the grounds that humans deserve protection too, they also demonstrated that they do care about animals. In a symbolic action, they handed over a stray dog to the FP representative, arguing that Hungerit had been a donor to animal shelters, a donation they claimed would be jeopardized should the boycott continue.

What is more, there would be an unintended consequence of a Europe-wide ban on foie gras production, one that clearly runs against the principles of the animal rights organizations. Without a consonant ban on the sale of fattened geese and duck liver, China would fill the sudden vacuum in foie gras supply; and, unlike Hungary or France, China has no animal protection laws. The effects of existing bans are already felt in China. A Chinese goose farmer was quoted by National Public Radio, "Because they're opposing foie gras, their countries stop producing it. But the citizens of their countries still want to eat foie gras, so it can only mean my prospects are improving." The report then sums up the prospects: "And with labor, feed and production costing just a fraction of what they would overseas [i.e., in Europe], he believes China is set to be the world's top foie gras producer in five years."[6] According to this argument, it is better to keep foie gras production, or any livestock-based industry, in Europe, where animals enjoy an ever-increasing set of legal protections. This unintended consequence highlights how ethical policies within a nation-state or even in a supranational organization have global implications and thus should also be molded by a larger context. In sum, using the analytics of the test of substantive legitimacy, Four Paws could not expect its Hungarian campaign to be legitimate.

Another test of legitimacy has to do not with substance but with process and procedure, asking whether the NGO in question operates in a way that fulfills its substantive principles. In Hungarian debates on the foie gras blacklist, I found that even people who otherwise would be sympathetic to the substantive argument about the inhumanity of force-feeding found the actual steps and modus operandi of Four Paws objectionable. To understand this it is useful to review the sequence of events here. In August 2008, a representative of Four Paws sat down to negotiate with the Hungarian Ministry of Agriculture (Földművelésügyi és Vidékfejlesztési Minisztérium, FVM) and representatives of the Hungarian poultry industry. The meeting was productive insofar as it came up with a solution in which the producers and the FVM agreed (a) to labeling of fattened poultry products, indicating that they result from force-feeding, while asserting that the fattening process is in compliance with Hungarian laws, (b) to elaborate and legislate a code on proper feeding techniques, (c) to monitor animal welfare in the presence of representatives of civic animal rights organizations, and (d) to contribute to a research and development program for changing the fattening technology. In return, they requested that (a) Four Paws suspend its blacklist for a period to be agreed upon, (b) future blacklists designate products rather than companies, (c) FP cooperate in designing regulations, (d) FP support the research and development program and technological change financially and with expertise, and (e) FP use its influence to contribute to the positive image of firms that have adopted these new technologies. In addition, Hungerit, as I mentioned, ceased its foie gras production for the duration of these negotiations (September 2008 to January 2009) as a show of good faith.

Despite this agreement, FP never eliminated the blacklist, and instead of implementing the agreement, it asked for (and received) the resignation of the employee who had represented it in the negotiations, a move that almost derailed the communication between poultry interests and FP.[7] Four Paws argued that labeling that marks fattening as in accordance with Hungarian laws misleads consumers, because, according to the group, Hungarian food laws prohibit the force-feeding of animals in general but allow it for the manufacturing of fattened poultry products.[8] FVM nevertheless did go through with legislating its labeling law, which is now in force.

Some people and organizations have criticized FP on procedural grounds, for (a) blacklisting firms (and all their products) rather than just fattened poultry commodities, (b) targeting producers only in Hungary, a country whose farmer lobby has been weak, (c) taking liberties in "documenting" (see below) and then reporting animal abuse on geese farms to the media, (d) its conduct in negotiations with the FVM and poultry sector representatives, especially its previously mentioned withdrawal from the initial agreement, and (e) a lack of transparency in the sources of its information and funding.

FP argues that it does target French foie gras producers as well, though my search of English-language sources, including reports put out by the organization itself, have revealed no active campaign at the time of writing.[9] A farmers' movement such as the one represented by Jose Bové— the French farmer who has led a successful campaign against neoliberal globalization and various multinational corporations in defense of small farmers' autonomy—would have been too formidable an enemy and would have alienated a potential ally in campaigns against industrial animal husbandry. France also presents a harder nut to crack for FP, because foie gras is much more integrated into the daily diet there than anywhere else in the world. The only possible indication of FP having tried to effect change in France is that their video documenting the cruelty of force-feeding shows ducks being fed with metal tubes. According to the head of the Hungarian veterinarians' alliance, in Hungary farmers only use rubber tubes and ducks represent only a small proportion of Hungarian

foie gras production. That also means that the video documenting the discarding of male offspring is unlikely to have been taken in Hungary—and
more likely to have been shot in France—because both sexes of the goose
species raised on Hungarian farms can be used for fattening.

Several Hungarian TV programs have pointed out these inconsistencies in FP's documentary evidence and criticized the group for not appearing on programs after having promised they would.[10] Furthermore, when
their videos showed obvious animal abuse, they refused to disclose where
they were recorded, as for example in their more recent campaign against
feather plucking. The Hungarian animal rights organization Fehérkereszt
also charged that if FP does not disclose where such practices took place,
it itself aids and abets animal torture and thus is guilty itself.[11]

Therefore, Four Paws' campaign fails to satisfy either the substantive
or the procedural criteria of legitimacy. While Four Paws may not be
thinking in terms of these exact analytical criteria, we are now in a much
better position to understand why it has had to frame its actions in terms
of other, this time more widely accepted moral arguments. One such argument is about foie gras being a luxury product. FP hopes that when
one weighs the alleged harm of gavage against the luxury and gourmet
tastes of a narrow rich consumer elite, one is likely to come out against
force-feeding. As we will see, Hungarian public opinion tends to connect
foie gras production not with elite consumption but with Hungarian traditions. The argument about sinful consumption may, however, work for
individuals already critical of the nouveau riche, consumerism, and social
inequalities in general.

The second argument is about for-profit animal husbandry. In a similar
way to the first moral claim, FP balances animal torture against profits
made by foie gras producers. While goose liver is an expensive product,
and while processors tend to realize a higher profit rate on it than on other
poultry products, raising geese is also a much more labor-intensive process than, for example, industrial chicken production. Goose feed is more
expensive than factory feed for broiler chickens, and the feeding itself has
to be very precise, both in terms of portions and timing. When geese are
fattened, they become fragile and require extreme care in feeding and han-
dling. These extra expenses lead to high prices. At the same time, however,
public opinion does not weigh the image of geese being force-fed against

the image of profits and dollar signs, but against struggling farmers, so that this is an unlikely moral claim to win.

The third frame is ideological in content but gains its power from the moral condemnation of the communist past. Markus Miller, director of Four Paws' international campaign against foie gras production, made the following claim: "The [Hungarian poultry] industry is divided into those who are oriented towards the future and those who are lost in the dark past of communism" (FP press release 2008). But as the previous moral claims about luxury consumption and profit motives suggest, FP also distances itself from capitalism, at least from French and Israeli capital: "Hungarian poultry producers are enslaved by French and Israeli investors, who mislead Hungarian producers and force employees to work for minimum wage so they can increase their profits and abandon them in a destroyed environment and leave them with the infamy of animal torture" (FP press release 2008). While this may read like a sympathetic embrace of the workers and farmers, it elides the opinion of many Hungarians that at present it is a single animal rights organization, Four Paws, that is bent on destroying this "environment" and on stigmatizing Hungarian agriculture. This leaves FP's empathy for the poor without credibility in the eyes of the Hungarian public.

FP's simultaneous identification of pro–foie gras interests with Israel and communism angers people sensitive to anti-Semitism (evoking the right-wing conviction that communism in Hungary was a Jewish conspiracy). While several informants made the charge that FP reminds them of Nazis—German Nazis had their dances with vegetarianism and with organic agriculture—I suspect a more pragmatic motivation behind FP's allegedly anti-Semitic rhetoric. In the media FP has repeatedly been represented as anti-Hungarian or representing the interests of a firm affiliated with a powerful German chain, so FP must have felt compelled to try to take the wind out of the sails of that argument. Its failure on the substantive test of NGO legitimacy created a further incentive for FP to appear more pro-Hungarian. For example, while in a TV interview that aired in Germany, FP advised Western consumers to buy German or Polish free range poultry instead of Hungarian foie gras, in addressing Hungarian audiences, it talked about Hungary restoring its "fame as the EU's most professional and most successful agricultural member state" (*Szempont*

2008). FP accesses a familiar patriotic rhetoric when it references *Hungarian* farmers, *Hungarian* workers, and *Hungarian* consumers all cheated by the poultry industry. The next section will analyze how this "nationalization" of the debate on foie gras played itself out on both sides.

As we have seen, transnational social relations play contradictory roles in postsocialist moral restructuring: while there is a transfer of western European ethical attitudes through corporate social responsibility and the adoption of strict animal rights standards, this process deprives some Hungarian actors not merely of the right to hold distinct moral convictions, but also of the liberal subject's assumed capacity to act ethically.

Renationalizing Ethics

Hungarianness indeed has become a key trope in the debate. The pro–foie gras side utilizes a different moral frame, which accomplishes two tasks: it provides a positive redefinition of Hungarian foie gras production, and it discredits Four Paws. The FVM and the poultry industry have responded with a savvy PR campaign. The PR firm in charge of the campaign also has established a web page (hungarikum.org) that gives information about the history and practices of foie gras production and forcefully makes the argument that "[i]n Hungary *gavage* is a several hundred years-long tradition already mentioned in written records from the twelfth century. Fattened goose is a unique Hungarian meal; goose breeding and raising and the distinctive expertise on which these are based has been elaborated over centuries.... This kind of expertise and uniqueness is also recognized and regulated by the European Union" (http://www.hungarikum.org/a-hizottliba-mint-hungarikum.html, last accessed June 22, 2009).

Hungary has taken its cues in this campaign from France, which designated foie gras as part of its national cultural heritage and drew up two protections for it: EU designation as "traditional specialty guaranteed" (as possessed by Bordeaux wine), and *label rouge* (for free-range products), which accrues to some foie gras labels. Indeed, in Hungary's case as well, it is the culturalization or ethnicization of foie gras that has proved to be the most influential argument against FP. The foie gras of Orosháza was already designated as a Hungaricum—a unique product (typically food or drink) whose special quality, fame, or know-how ties it to Hungary. The pro–foie gras campaign also put out videos on the subject peppered with national symbols and folk music.[12]

In 2009 the foie gras product of Hungerit received the "Excellent Hungarian Product" award. Recipients of this award are not only entitled to use the logo of this award in their advertisements and packaging, but they can also receive financial and marketing assistance for the award-winning product. The marketing agency operated by the agricultural ministry allocated additional funds for a PR and advertising campaign targeting German and Austrian markets in 2009. They also released a video showing how fattening is actually done.[13]

The positive redefinition of foie gras therefore consists of the following arguments:

(a) force-feeding is not animal torture but an animal husbandry technique;

(b) this technique has deep roots in Hungarian folklore and culinary traditions;

(c) foie gras is a high-quality agricultural export product that contributes positively to the image of Hungary abroad;

(d) foie gras production keeps the already much-emaciated Hungarian food industry afloat (as mentioned in the introductory chapter, it is one of a handful of food products in which Hungary has managed to increase its share of the world trade since the collapse of state socialism and EU accession); and

(e) goose fattening is a regulated and monitored activity, and its regulation is based on veterinarian expertise and is in compliance with current EU regulations.

In addition to the positive moral valuation of Hungarian foie gras, the FVM and the poultry industry have also presented Four Paws as a corrupt entity. Besides the above-mentioned critiques of the FP campaign, they argue that FP lacks an existential moral ground to make its claims credible. As the head of the Poultry Product Council put it, "Their average age is less than 27, they have no work experience, no life experience, they never had to pay their own utility bills, they never had to buy school milk for their kids or a bus pass for their kids. At the same time it seems to me they consider this a big party [jó buli]."[14]

The enemy image of a young and well-to-do urban professional kept resurfacing in the pro–foie gras rhetoric. "Let's defend our Hungarianness and everything that belongs to it. Or shall we allow a handful of ignoramuses *sitting in their leather armchairs* to soil our values and destroy the lives of thousands, while taking no responsibility?!"[15] In the visual representation of this male character—in a slideshow on the hungarikum.org web page—we see the added feature of violent anger, which represents an especially stark contrast with the pastoral pictures of geese in meadows and of elderly farmers with anxious faces, gently cuddling geese eggs and hatchlings.

Struggles for Moral Sovereignty

It might seem that the poultry industry mobilizes Hungarianness in a manipulative way in its rhetoric against FP. What makes this case in my mind transcend usual stories of exploiting national pride on behalf of industrial interests, however, is not simply the mentioned surveys indicating that the majority sees foie gras as a traditional Hungarian culinary product and the boycott as an attack on the nation's economy. The transnational context of this case, and especially how that context is viewed by the Hungarian public and political parties, in effect makes it inevitable that the campaign is viewed primarily in a national framing. In social science literature, the alternative to identity politics is class politics, also referred to as a politics of (re)distribution as opposed to one of recognition (Fraser 1997; Fraser and Honneth 2003; Taylor 1994; Young 1990). In theory, therefore, parties and politicians of leftist leanings could have discussed the boycott as an attack on poor small farmers (one of the biggest losers of EU accession), but this would have required that the same politicians be able to name not just the victims but the "victimizers." Since in this case those who occupy the top layer of social hierarchy of the agricultural spectrum—the food processing companies—shared the interest of the small farmers, class politics could not be contained domestically. To the extent that the alleged perpetrators were the German food industry and an Austrian animal rights organization, framing the case in terms of class would have required the left to take up the issue of East-West economic inequalities. The Hungarian Socialist Party (Magyar Szocialista Párt, MSZP) was reluctant to do that. Not only did the left-liberal parties implement or support neoliberal reforms, but they also fully supported EU membership. The liberal and left-wing parties, who elsewhere are the greatest champions of pro-poor policies, in the postsocialist context abandoned the issue of internationally derived economic inequalities, thus ceding that terrain to their conservative right-wing counterparts, who naturally framed such inequalities in national terms. In that framing, the collective that needs protection is not a class, but the nation as a whole, and the enemy is a homogenously rendered image of the West. It is this shared sense of victimization of the nation as a whole that is reflected in the poultry industry's rhetoric against Four Paws.

This national collective is made up of the Hungarian agrarium: the countryside, the farmers, and the workers who depend on foie gras for their livelihood. Following Katherine Verdery (1994), who argues that the moral and political capital earned by victims of communism becomes a key resource in postcommunist legislative and political struggles, I would argue that a similarly powerful victimhood narrative has been forged based on the post-1989 experience. This time victimhood develops in relation to powerful foreign actors, such as the EU, the World Bank, NATO, the WTO, and the IMF, for all of which the lay term is simply "the West." It is this seemingly omnipotent agent that, in the minds of most Hungarian farmers, has pulled the rug out from under Hungarian agriculture, first by opening up domestic markets to Western food products; then by denying or reducing farmer subsidies allotted by the Common Agricultural Policy that had been dangled as a carrot in front of the otherwise Euro-skeptical rural voters; and finally by using quality, safety, and animal rights standards to block Hungarian access to Western food markets. It is not just that most Hungarians consider animal rights a luxury at a time when unemployment and poverty are increasing (especially since the 2008 financial crisis) and when small farms are rapidly disappearing. More importantly, the accusation of animal torture places farmers in the position of perpetrators and thus damages, if not destroys, the moral shelter of victimhood. When it is a Western animal rights organization that engages in stigmatizing a traditional Hungarian agricultural practice—and its Hungarian counterpart, White Cross, disagrees—there is a profound sense of infringement on the nation's moral sovereignty.

Indeed, the concept of moral sovereignty evoked by the new Polish government in 2006 in demanding a greater role for Catholicism in EU politics rested on the nation. The official Polish position forcefully pushed for the recognition of European culture's Christian origins, fearing that without such recognition the government's ethical stance on various issues, especially abortion, would lose its legitimacy in the eyes of an overall more secular and liberal Europe. In that instance, moral sovereignty accrued to the nation as a whole, and its invocation expressed an objection to longstanding tendencies to orientalize eastern Europe.

The question of moral sovereignty in the foie gras case, however, is not simply an issue of whether FP's ethical values are consistent with Hungarian ones; that is, the experience of infringement of Hungarians' moral sovereignty does not simply imply that national sovereignty was violated in a moral sense. Moral sovereignty here, rather, accrues to a class of people who presently are still seen as the producers and guards of Hungarian identity and cultural tradition: the farmers.[16] We will understand this better if we inspect the collective in FP's notion of the common good. FP here is closer to the liberal notion of public, insofar as it references European social norms and the regulation, that is, the banning, of foie gras production in many European countries. It is however not alone in this framing. People in a middle position, critiquing FP's particular modus operandi but also attracted to a less industrial, more alternative vision of food production, argue that the foie gras industry knew this was coming and should have behaved more proactively to decrease its vulnerability, both to animal rights charges and to a possible ban on foie gras production by the EU. They argue that Hungarian meat processors should have decreased their reliance on a handful of Western buyers and diversified their products and their clientele, and that they should have looked into changing technology for raising geese earlier. This framing, defining the industry and the farmers not as victims but as capable economic actors, echoes ideas of neoliberal governmentality and its demand for and production of a self-governing, rational actor fully responsible for his or her actions.

The obstacle to goose farmers assuming this subject position, however, is double. First, as soon as they present themselves as rationally acting in their self-interest, they confirm FP's arguments about the selfish profit motivation for animal cruelty. Second, the concept of the neoliberal subject presupposes a degree of control, choice, and ability to exercise citizenship rights. But at a time when EU policies "strongly encourage" farmers to leave agriculture, when farmers have no control over whom to sell their products to and at what price, when they are less and less capable of holding on to their land due to land prices ratcheted up by the impending end of the ban on foreign land ownership, when they are forced to implement safety and quality standards originally designed for industrial animal husbandry and food processing (Mincyte 2011, 2012; Dunn 2005), it is highly questionable whether they will be able to leave the only subject position they have available to themselves: that of *Hungarian* victims.

This sense of victimhood, however, is fomented not only by what may seem a nationalist politics of grievance. Indeed, it is moored in concrete practices, even though these are entirely ignored by Four Paws.

ETHICS AS PRACTICE

Social constructivists readily admit that what is ethical is in the eye of the beholder, that different cultures disagree about what constitutes ethical behavior. We are more reluctant to go further and recognize that these different ethical norms arise from different material practices. Bruno Latour (2002) argues that certain bans, taboos, or ethical norms are put in place "to slow us down on our way" to a certain desired outcome. That is, it is not so much the outcome of a practice, but rather the way and ease with which we get there that needs to be regulated by ethical surveillance. Indeed, most contemporary ethical consumption movements call not for banning commodities, but for consuming commodities produced in a particular way. Ethically produced coffee, for example, is coffee grown by farmers in environmentally and socially sustainable ways (Lyon and Moberg 2010). Similarly, anti–foie gras activists condemn not the consumption of duck or goose liver, but the material practices that currently yield foie gras. An American anti–foie gras chef, for example, argued in no less a spectacular venue than ted.com that it is possible to make foie gras without force-feeding and with an ecologically sustainable open ranch method that he encountered and personally tested in Spain (Barber 2008). It is therefore clear that what constitutes ethical consumption in this case is the consumption of foie gras produced in a particular way.[17]

The framing of ethics in this campaign was problematic because it was based on the assumption that these practices were the same in Hungary as in the countries where the boycott and movement had originated. While this may reflect the coming future of globalization, which has indeed produced standardization tendencies in many industries, with Hungarian foie gras this was not the case.

The Production Process and Animal Living Conditions

In Hungary it is mainly geese, and only very rarely ducks, that are fattened through gavage. Eggs are hatched in large-scale hatcheries, from which farmers usually buy the goslings at four weeks of age. Until nine weeks of age geese are raised in relatively natural conditions and spend ample time outdoors. On the family farm I visited in Kiskunfélegyháza, geese had a huge barn all to themselves and the barn itself was wide open on two ends, so that the young geese could freely go in and out. After nine weeks, usually at another farm, they started to be fattened. During this stage, which lasted two to three weeks, geese lived in relative confinement because too much movement would make them lose weight.

I observed two different spatial arrangements for barns set up for gavage. On the farm at Kiskunfélegyháza the barn had about ten pens, each approximately two by two meters, the whole barn containing about twenty geese. The barn had low ceilings, probably not much higher than two meters. Geese could move around within the pens. The ground was covered with hay, and doors and windows were open. This family had another barn of this size for geese undergoing gavage, and at any given time they said they had 200 to 250 geese total, the majority still in the pregavage phase. I watched the geese being led out of the pens to the feeder located in the corner, where they would usually "line up," but since they were afraid of strangers they piled themselves in the corner, tucking their heads into each others' wings. The male head of the household was in charge of feeding that day. He grabbed a goose by the neck and swiftly and smoothly opened its beak and positioned it on the rubber feeding tube. He then turned on a machine that pumps the measured batches of feed into the throats of the birds for three seconds or so. After that he let the goose go, who then waddled back to its pen with its wings wide open, loudly honking on the way.

At another family farm I visited in Kiskunmajsa, which takes care of four hundred geese at any one time, the birds were kept in what seemed more cramped and what I would describe as less comfortable conditions. Here the barn was much bigger and had higher ceilings, and overall it seemed darker and smelled worse. The barn was divided into rows of stainless steel cages raised about a meter off the ground. The cages had no tops, so the birds' necks were above the top railing of the cage. Each cage measured about one by two meters and contained three to four geese. Here it was the feeder (again the adult man of the household) who moved around, rather than the geese coming to him. As he went along each row of cages, he pulled with him the tube that was suspended from the ceiling by elastic cables and attached to the feed-mixing machine. The geese were exactly at hand level to the feeder, and since the cages had holes on the bottom, as did the floor, feces were meant to just drop through both. Nevertheless, there were still some feces stuck to the bottom bars of the cages. When the feeder appeared, the geese showed signs of excitement.[18] They turned toward the feeder and started honking loudly. According to the feeder and his wife, this is how the birds demand to be fed. They echoed other farmers' views that geese get used to being force-fed and after about three to four days even start demanding feeding. They get fed like this twice a day.

The farms presented a very different image of the raising and feeding of the birds than the model the animal rights organizations, such as Four Paws, have documented on video. Indeed, it seems that Four Paws only documented the worst types of practices, which indeed constitute abuse. First, in the Hungarian farms I visited, the birds spent a considerable part of their life outdoors and with a great amount of free movement. Second, the geese did not shake their heads, as seen in the video made in France, a behavior that is said to be a sign of hyperventilation caused by overfeeding. Another difference between the French and Hungarian practices— and not only the farms I visited—is that in Hungary only rubber tubes are used for gavage, rather than the metal ones shown in the video. This innovation is a Hungarian one. According to the director of the Hungarian Veterinary Association, it makes the feeding less painful for the birds and is obligatory for every producer in the country. In Hungary, only geese are force-fed. Unlike ducks—which constitute the majority of birds fattened through gavage in France—in the case of geese both sexes can be fattened. This is significant because one especially cruel practice, according to video posted by antigavage activists, is live male ducklings being disposed of in a grinder. If indeed only or mostly geese are fattened in Hungary, then we would not expect live birds to be disposed of in this way (or at all).

This however does not mean that I have no concerns about animal welfare in the Hungarian cases. While the need to limit the birds' movement in the last three weeks of their lives is understandable, I think that the tightness of space in the second type of facility may not have been necessary. After all, the geese at the first farm had more room, which had no negative effect on their weight. Furthermore, in the second farm's practices, it is likely that the bars on the bottom of the cage cut into the feet of the birds. (As mentioned, the bottom of the cages is uncovered so that feces can drop through, making the cleaning easier for the farmers.) To me, solid ground covered by hay that is regularly changed to keep the floor clean seems a more humane setting.

Of course FP itself could have made such an evaluation if it had based its campaign on the actual practices in the country, but it instead opted for using the same campaign video animal rights activists used elsewhere. The lack of local knowledge was made particularly spectacular when the leader of FP's campaign, appearing on a Hungarian television talk show, could not even tell the difference between a duck and a goose.

Anti–foie gras activists reduce ethics to particular aspects of the socio-material assemblage that makes up goose raising and foie gras production. For FP the key aspect of this assemblage is the interaction between the human (the farmer) and the nonhuman (the bird). The hand of the farmer seems to commit an act of violence in pushing food down the throat of the bird. But, as I witnessed in Kiskunfélegyháza, the hand of the farmer also pets and cuddles the bird before, during, and after the few seconds it takes for him to administer the batch of grains. The hand of the farmer also checks for signs of injury or disease regularly, diagnoses problems, and applies cures if necessary. I am not idealizing the goose farmer as some kind of a noble savage. I am simply pointing out that there is more to the human-bird interaction than that implied in the propaganda materials of the anti–foie gras campaign, which, for good reasons, attends only to some aspects of this contact. We could also extend our gaze to the outer reaches of this sociomaterial assemblage, namely the livelihoods that raising geese affords. The hand that interacts with the birds, to wit, is also a hand that shops, cooks, tidies, and in numerous other ways sustains a family and a community. To sever the few seconds of interaction between goose and farmer during feeding times from this larger assemblage is to make possible a certain social, legal, and political interpretation of foie gras production. In the two concluding chapters of this book I will come back to the nature of this politics.

3

THE 2010
RED MUD SPILL

On October 4, 2010, seven hundred thousand cubic meters (24.7 million cubic feet) of toxic sludge escaped from pond number 10, a reservoir of an alumina factory owned by the Magyar Alumínium Termelő és Kereskedelmi Zrt. (MAL Ltd.), in western Hungary. The stream, which flooded three villages, was a twenty-five-kilometer-long, between one- and two-kilometer-wide, and occasionally over two-meter-high cascade of mud. Ten people, including a one-year-old infant, died from burns or drowning, and hundreds were treated in hospitals. More than two hundred houses that survived still had to be demolished. All life in the nearest river, the Marcal, a tributary of the Danube, was extinguished—fish, birds, insects, and plants. According to government officials, this was Hungary's worst-ever ecological disaster.

RED MUD

Red mud is the byproduct of alumina (aluminum oxide) production, the first step in producing aluminum. In the Bayer process, bauxite is treated with a caustic solution (sodium hydroxide, or NaOH) to remove impurities. This technology was developed in the late nineteenth century and, amazingly, is still the most-used process. The resulting waste has a low solid material content and is highly alkaline. The scientific literature puts its pH at a maximum of 12, but in Hungary the spilled slurry had a pH of 13–14, which due to the logarithmic nature of the pH scale is a significant difference. Red mud usually contains iron oxide (rust), aluminum oxide, calcium oxide, titanium oxide, sodium oxide, and silicon oxide. The actual composition of course depends on the characteristics of the ore used, but iron oxide is always the largest ingredient, and it is this component that lends red mud its color.

The production of one ton of alumina generates an average of one to two tons of red mud, depending on the quality or purity of the ore used, though the actual range is quite wide: between 0.3 and 2.5 tons (Jones and Haynes 2011). The Bayer technology thus operates with a high waste-to-final-product ratio. Red mud constitutes the second-largest category (not counting tailings from mining), at 23 percent, of worldwide industrial processing waste, with steel manufacturing at 70 percent making up the largest share (Cooling 2007). According to current estimates, by 2015 there will be four billion tons of bauxite residue (red mud) globally (Power, Gräfe, and Klauber 2009, iv).

This sludge is disposed of in two main ways. Where there is coastal access, it is dumped into the sea, a method that has been practiced at least in France, the UK, Germany, Greece, and Japan (Bánvölgyi and Huan n.d.; de Bois 2010; Red Mud Project n.d.).[1] More landlocked facilities instead have created lagoons or holding ponds for the sludge, which can then be dewatered and treated to a varying extent. Hungary, with no access to the sea, has been using this method for many decades. Until relatively recently there were three areas near various alumina facilities that hosted such lagoons: Almásfüzitő, near the Slovakian border; Mosonmagyaróvár, near the Austrian border, a site that has now been closed and reclaimed; and Ajka, in the northwest of the country, fifty kilometers north of Lake Balaton, the site that was the source of the 2010 disaster.

Wet deposition, the lagoon method, is essentially the traditional way of dealing with tailings from mines, and it is the cheapest way to dispose of red mud. The two key problems with this process are the high likelihood of seepage into the soil and groundwater, and the corrosion of the lagoon walls due to red mud's low viscosity and the continuous movement of the sludge in the impoundment (due to rain and wind), which may lead to the fracture of the walls and consequent flooding. What renders these two scenarios particularly dangerous is the high alkalinity, rather than the toxicity, of the material.

To mitigate such hazards, starting around 1980 most Western alumina factories shifted to disposal methods that reduce both the wetness and the alkalinity of red mud. The most common has been the so-called dry stacking method, in which underground drainage and the sloped spreading of the red mud allows it to dry to 70 percent solid content, after which another load can be piled on top. Increasing the solid content to an even higher level is not desirable because the dust thus generated spreads easily and presents a serious health hazard. People near the spill, for example, reported a burning sensation in their upper respiratory system after the spilled material started to dry out and the wind increased. Asthma symptoms also worsened, especially for children, according to an informant, who not only has three children but is also an elementary school teacher. The advantage of dry stacking is that the removal of the caustic liquid from the byproduct also decreases its alkalinity. Other methods of neutralization include adding seawater, which brings the pH level down to a range of 8.0–9.5. The problem with this method, however, is that it introduces salt and potentially other impurities into the leachate, which can endanger agriculture and drinking water sources. A more recent method, which avoids salination and can potentially reduce global greenhouse gas emissions, is carbonation. Here the sludge is suffused with carbon dioxide gas, bringing alkalinity down to a pH range of 9–10. Both methods are considered expensive, although according to the literature such expenditures are likely to be offset by savings on future remediation.

THE HUNGARIAN ALUMINUM INDUSTRY
AND THE HISTORY OF RED MUD

Ajka houses the largest alumina-producing facility in Hungary, its origins dating back to 1941. The Hungarian aluminum industry, however, only developed significantly after the communist takeover in 1948. The new government, in view of Hungary's lack of raw material resources necessary for heavy industry and energy generation, jumped at the chance to utilize the significant bauxite sources concentrated in the northwestern quadrant of the country. As an industry of utmost military and economic significance, its enterprises (the bauxite mines, alumina factories, smelters, and mills) were not only nationalized but, in 1950 were subsumed by a Hungarian-Soviet "joint venture" called Maszobal (Juhász 1977; Berend and Ránki 1985). This is hardly surprising: Hungary's share in the total bauxite production of the socialist bloc grew to a full one-third, necessitating direct Soviet supervision. The Soviet role did not disappear even after the Hungarian government bought out the Soviet partner in 1954; rather, in 1962 Hungary signed an agreement to send raw alumina to the Soviet Union and then bring the resulting aluminum back, allegedly to take advantage of cheaper energy for smelting.[2] The difference in price was paid either in Hungarian industrial products or in extra alumina. The two countries only agreed to end this barter in 1988, intending to transform it starting in 1990 into a more conventional business contract in which prices reflected the world market and were paid in cash. By this time, however, state socialism and the whole socialist economic bloc were crumbling. Before we look at the implications of this momentous transformation, let us understand the environmental regulations in place before and after 1989.

ENVIRONMENTAL REGULATION AS TRANSNATIONAL

There are ten holding ponds adjacent to the Ajka factory, and they were all established under state socialism, when the factory was state-owned. The lagoons were meant to store red mud and gray sludge. The latter is the tailing resulting from coal mining, and it was stored here because Ajka's power plant burns locally mined coal. At the time of the disaster there was an estimated volume of fifty million cubic meters of gray sludge and thirty million cubic meters of red mud stored in the ponds, and gray sludge had been used for building the impoundment walls of the more recent lagoons. Pond no. 10 was the tallest, with walls as high as twenty-five meters. As mentioned above, the key environmental hazard of lagoons such as these is their seepage, which indeed had been constant for the past several decades according to nearby villagers I interviewed. Another potential hazard is that sludge with high water content (and the red mud around Ajka had only a 50–60 percent solid content) can be moved about by winds, which weakens the walls of the impoundment over time.

One environmental installation that had been prescribed by the state and that MAL did complete was an underground buffer wall that was supposed to prevent seepage into the surrounding soil. This construction began in the early 1980s, and after its completion in 2001, it surrounded ponds nos. 6–9, with a length of 7.4 kilometers. According to MAL's representatives, however, this barrier, by allowing rainwater to pool around the lagoon's walls, ended up compromising the structural integrity of the dams. This was one instance when MAL pushed the blame back onto the state, and there were others. But according to other experts, a more significant cause of the walls' fracture was that they had been raised multiple times, thus increasing the pressure they had to withstand.[3] In order to understand the circumstances involving the storage of red mud, and specifically the height of the walls of pond no. 10, it is necessary to introduce both the national and local regulations.

Regulation on Different Scales

Hungary introduced its first hazardous waste policy in 1981, well before the collapse of state socialism. This classified waste into three categories of increasing dangerousness, and red mud was considered to be in the second category. Red mud constituted and still constitutes a high percentage of all hazardous waste—about 25 percent in 2000—which renders Hungary's waste composition unique among all industrial countries.[4]

Until 1979, the red mud around Ajka was neutralized by dewatering, which made it a material solid enough to be moved by shovel.[5] The amount of dry red mud transported by trucks to the disposal sites became prohibitively large and thus very expensive, at a time when energy prices were already at a record high; consequently, the dewatering process was stopped in favor of piping the more fluid wastes directly into the newer ponds. This in some sense brought or promised to bring an improvement in air quality, which had been spoiled by the dust blowing off the drying red mud sites. A Hungarian environmental sociologist, Viktória Szirmai, documented these problems in a report, citing both her informants and contemporary newspapers, that talked of a veritable red cloud hovering over the land (Szirmai and Lehocki 1988). According to her sources, visibility during windy weather was reduced to four to five meters.[6] But the newer ponds exacerbated another problem: leakage that, as tests would show, rendered drinking water from nearby wells unfit for human consumption and caused plants and trees to wither.

Szirmai and her colleague Zsuzsa Lehocki also analyzed the debates among the members of an ad hoc committee appointed by the municipal government [városi tanács] of Ajka and the Ajka alumina company, in which the height of the impoundment walls was the most contested issue. According to the environmental authorities, the company had a permit for a height of sixteen meters, but in its plans for increasing the capacity of the holding ponds it was referring to wall heights of twenty-five to forty meters. Given that, according to the committee, nowhere in Europe did walls exceed nine meters, one can understand the local concerns, among which the danger of dam failure loomed large. The local political committee of the party and the alumina factory, however, shared an interest in increasing capacity by elevating the pond walls rather than by establishing new lagoons, which would have taken huge areas of land out of agricultural cultivation. So eventually, her report concludes, the municipal government stopped representing the citizenry's environmental interests and issued the permits for elevating the walls.

At the same time, the older, already full ponds were left without plant covering,[7] and in addition, seepage continued through the decade, both from the newer ponds and even from the formerly dewatered ones, for example after heavy rains. Nevertheless, the fact that red mud was classified as hazardous waste allowed for stricter monitoring, which, even if not religiously carried out under state socialism, provided the alumina producer with incentives to comply. This was the kind of oversight that led to the formation of the ad hoc committee in the first place and that allowed the burgeoning of a new literature on hazardous wastes in Hungary, which in turn supplied the committee with the information about other countries' practices, including the usual dam heights in Europe.

According to MAL, however, the socialist state had made another mistake by allowing pond no. 10 to be built in that particular location. Two different kinds of soil substrates meet at the edge of this particular reservoir, causing differential reactions in the foundation to pressure and precipitation, thus causing cracks in the walls of the lagoon. For years, university professors in engineering have been teaching the case of these reservoirs to their students as a negative example of where not to site a waste facility, not only because of the soil conditions but also because of its proximity to residential areas, to rivers that flow into the Danube, and to drinking water sources.[8] The Parliamentary Committee investigating the disaster, however, rejected the presence of different soil substrates as being the main cause of the dam failure (Jávor and Hargitai 2011).[9]

Western Regulation of Red Mud

One expectation of democratization and EU membership was that Hungary would adopt stricter environmental regulations and would improve the quality of air, water, and soil. Indeed, Hungary adopted a number of international waste regulations after the collapse of state socialism.

Already in 1989 it signed the Basel Convention—implementing it in 1992—according to which red mud is hazardous, no matter what its actual pH levels are. Other regulations applying to most European countries include Seveso I and II, dating from 1982 and 1996 respectively, which target prevention and preparation for industrial disasters;[10] the EU Mining Waste Directive 2006, which however doesn't apply to nonhazardous materials; REACH 2007 (Registration, Evaluation, Authorisation and Restriction of Chemicals); and the IPPC (Integrated Pollution Prevention and Control) Directive (2008), which in 2010 changed its name to the Industrial Emissions Directive (IED).

By the time Hungary was getting ready to enter the European Union in the early 2000s, alumina producers in the western European countries had mostly shifted to more advanced disposal methods that, as mentioned, resulted in a drier and less alkaline byproduct. Consequently, the European Union's Waste Code, in contrast to the Basel Convention, does not explicitly consider red mud a hazardous waste. In preparation for adopting the Environmental Acquis (the set of conditions for EU membership in the realm of environmental policy), Hungary adopted the EU's waste classification, although, as it later turned out, the Hungarian government could have retained the older classification without violating EU policy.

So why did the Hungarian environmental authorities fail to retain the hazardous waste classification for red mud? One response lies at the empirical level of regulatory changes, and many analysts of the case have focused on this. The friction resulted in part from the timing of regulatory changes such as the harmonization of Hungarian and EU environmental laws. The actual implementation or legal harmonization of environmental regulation created a kind of a loophole, whereby for a limited time the task of classifying the waste was up to the producer. In effect, MAL ended up declaring to the Hungarian state that its red mud was not hazardous waste. This was not simply self-regulation; it was self-diagnosis and self-interested interpretation of the law.[11]

Further complicating the issue of classification is that, according to MAL, red mud is not a waste product but an intermediary material in the aluminum production process. As a result, company representatives still do not consider the ponds at Ajka to be waste disposal sites, but rather production sites, in which the filtering of red mud and the recuperation of the caustic NaOH solution take place; that is to say, materials are not simply moved and left there, but materials (NaOH) are also taken out. If a site is to be a disposal site in the technical sense, it should only have a one-way material flow: into but not out of the ponds. Instead MAL called the ponds a "technological facility" [*technológiai berendezés*], and in its response to the Parliamentary Committee's report, company representatives insisted that a red mud lagoon does not become a disposal site until after it is closed for good. Occupying such a liminal status leaves open two contradictory definitions of the lagoons: from a technical perspective a stage in production, while from a regulatory perspective a disposal site.

Not only are the lagoons not dump sites, but neither is red mud toxic, according to MAL. The company and many of the experts it relies on still argue that red mud is not hazardous, it is simply extremely alkaline. In Hungarian the word toxic is usually translated as *mérgező*, which means poisonous. Clearly, MAL argues, red mud is not going to poison one on contact, but one should avoid skin contact with it; for example, "one should not bathe or swim in it," as the CEO said on the day of the catastrophe—to the outrage of villagers (*HVG* 2010).

In essence, responses to the question of why red mud was not classified as hazardous waste focus on regulations, blaming the incompetence of Hungarian environmental authorities for (allegedly) misinterpreting international policies and laws. For some this incompetence argument is complemented, and for others replaced, by the corruption argument, the fusing of economic and regulatory power. It is true that MAL's owners had connections to the top ranks of the Hungarian Socialist Party, which has been in and out of government for the previous twenty-five years. It is also true that the managed privatizations within the alumina industry in the 1990s favored former ministry officials such as Árpád Bakonyi, as well as the circle around the infamous Ferenc Gyurcsány, who would serve as Hungary's prime minister between 2004 and 2009.[12] Though this response is not incorrect from a factual perspective, in my view it short-cuts the analysis. The other answer to the hows and whys of classifying red mud lies at a deeper structural level and in the practical aspects of the harmonization of the EU's and Hungary's environmental regulation.

ENVIRONMENTAL REGULATION AS PRACTICE

In order to understand the material conditions under which red mud was regulated, it is useful to reflect on two policy views on industrial waste in the European Union. One sees waste as pollution, which requires safe disposal and treatment facilities. The other sees waste as potentially useful material that may be recovered for new future uses, which requires legal and economic incentives as well as technologies for reuse and recycling. The EU doesn't prescribe whether to reuse or dump a particular waste material in industry, though in the realm of consumer waste, it prescribes a minimum ratio of recycling. For example, its law on packaging waste called on all member countries to have between 55 and 80 percent of their packaging waste recycled by no later than December 31, 2008. In industry, the decision is left to individual producers, and in the context of a market economy, economic incentives will of course play a major role in choosing between recycling and disposal. Beyond this, in the specific context of postsocialist countries, a further deciding factor is who bears the costs of disposal, the state that once owned the factory that produced the waste, or the newly privatized company. This is far from being trivial; environmental technologies and cleanup costs could make or break the deal the State Privatization Agency made with the new owners. To understand this we need to go beyond the understanding of postsocialist privatization that focused, as the mainstream media did, on the owners' identity and political connections. We need to see it instead as a deep structural transformation of postsocialist societies.

Privatization and Ownership of the Red Mud Lagoons

In 1997, the Ajka Alumina Factory (Ajkai Timföldgyár) became the property of the Magyar Alumínium Termelő és Kereskedelmi Zrt. (MAL Ltd.), a private corporation that eventually vertically integrated almost all Hungarian bauxite and alumina processing and later even bought other eastern European plants. This was in large part necessary to survive the exhaustion of Hungarian bauxite resources. The actual process of privatizing all the state-owned enterprises in the aluminum industry started in 1995 and is a long and complicated story, with multiple name changes and selling and buying of plants, that is not relevant here. Suffice it to say that while initially the state resisted privatization due to the importance of the industry for Hungary's trade balance, the first half of the 1990s saw a severe drop in aluminum prices, which suddenly tipped the balance in favor of selling. The state, however, did not give up all interest in the future of the industry. The privatization agency in charge of the sale gave preference to Hungarian bidders over foreign ones, with the argument that foreign owners would only want to close these factories and flood the market with their products manufactured elsewhere, a practice that by then had become common all over the postsocialist world. In fact, one of the conditions of the privatization was that the company would continue production and not lay off people for the foreseeable future. The new owner, Árpád Bakonyi, was the former board chairman, appointed by the state just before the privatization commenced, which indicates a familiar case of "managed privatization" (Jávor and Hargitai 2011; Bockman 2011). The managed aspect refers to not announcing an open bid, or specifying the bid in such a way that only certain bidders or a particular person could be brought in as the new owner. This is in contrast to the competition that allegedly characterizes free market economies.

At the time of the disaster, three-fourths of MAL's production was being exported to western Europe, but, in part due to the economic crisis, it had been operating at a deficit. MAL representatives cited this fact to justify not having completed some of the environmental investments prescribed in the privatization contract. To understand this obligation, we must review the relationship between environmental policies and privatization in Hungary.

In the first postsocialist Hungarian privatizations up to 1992, the new owner typically received a guarantee that the state would clean up whatever environmental damage was later discovered. In some cases this cost exceeded the price of the firm, thus eliminating the state's income from privatizations. In addition, the amount and time limit of this guarantee were not subject to expert assessment, but were simply based on a bargain between seller and buyer. While a 1992 law ended this situation, it did not apply to so-called partial privatizations. In these, state enterprises' most profitable and cleanest plants were privatized, while those with deficits and environmental problems were left in the hands of the state, thus leaving the cleanup costs to those units that could least afford to pay them.

The complex process of privatizations in the Hungarian alumina industry created a situation of partial privatization, as a result of which the red mud ponds that had been decommissioned remained in state ownership, while the ones still in use, such as those around Ajka, were transferred to the new owner. The contract estimated the environmental remediation costs of these transferred ponds at 3.3 billion forints, which was used to justify the ridiculously low sale price of 10 million forints for assets estimated by the Parliamentary Committee, based on company records, to be worth 1,591,040 million forints (Jávor and Hargitai 2011).[13] Intentionally undervaluing assets to be privatized in return for kickbacks was another common practice in postsocialist denationalization and was a likely cause of the low sale price in this case as well. The contract obliged the new owner to send annual reports to the privatization agency on the progress made in environmental remediation, and it threatened financial sanctions should the new owner fail to invest the prescribed sum in environmental projects. This penalty, however, was again so low (10 percent of the value of the damage caused) that it could not help but make it rational for MAL to ignore the terms of the contract.

The significance of privatization for the red mud storage at Ajka, however, goes beyond the company's privatization. Privatization in a larger social context was (a) a mechanism to redistribute wealth, (b) a process of capital accumulation, since redistribution in reality led to a concentration of assets, (c) the weakening of the state's economic power, and (d) the ascendance of the profit motive to the supreme rationale of all economic activity. These factors were combined in the red mud case. The transfer of the alumina industry into private hands weakened the government, and not only in the sense described above, namely by shortchanging the state. Low state income from privatizations also had the cumulative effect of siphoning off resources from, among other things, regulatory enforcement. As detailed in *From the Cult of Waste to the Trash Heap of History* (Gille 2007), not only was there an overall tendency to deregulate after 1989, but the staff and monetary resources available to environmental authorities were also severely depleted. Both circumstances are known from the scholarship to create favorable conditions for regulatory incompetence and corruption.

The simultaneous concentration of capital in turn increased the leverage of MAL's new owners, several of whom are counted among Hungary's twenty richest citizens. As we know from the literature on Western capitalist countries, such economic powerhouses can seriously impede the state's ability and willingness to monitor their activities, even in the absence of explicit bribery or other forms of corruption. It is usually sufficient for such interests to cite their contributions to local and national taxes and share of employment in order to get a free pass on many regulatory issues.

There is indeed evidence that there were serious shortcomings in both regulation and monitoring in this case. Of the several instances of governance failure, I would emphasize two. First, almost all the authorities, ranging from the local to the national, that potentially could have had a say in the operation and the monitoring of the lagoons, when interviewed by the Parliamentary Committee investigating the case, claimed a lack of authority. This impotence resulted from the uncertainty around the categorization of red mud: whether it is waste, whether it is toxic, whether it is hazardous, and whether regulatory oversight over this material is exercised by the mining or environmental authorities, as mentioned above. It was also unclear who was responsible for checking the walls' integrity, the composition and toxicity of the red mud, the production process, and the contamination of soil and groundwater. It is telling that just two weeks before the catastrophe, the on-site examination of the lagoons by the regional environmental inspectorate found everything in order—an inspection that did not, however, extend to examining the structural integrity of the ponds. Ironically, under one of the socialist governments, MAL had even received the "For Our Environment" award from the Environmental Ministry.

Second, both the mechanism by which the national level regulatory agencies could have determined whether the nonhazardous categorization of the alumina byproduct was correct and the actual monitoring of the fulfillment of the environmental requirements of the privatization were absent. This too points to a lack of coordination among various authorities.

While state ownership in itself is no guarantee of better environmental performance, as the track record of state socialism indicates, it is generally true that state-owned enterprises have what János Kornai (1980) has called soft(er) budget constraints. In practice that means that the profit motive can be subordinated to other objectives, such as maintaining state control in an industry of strategic or security significance, providing lower prices to consumers, and higher employment. In fact, all three of these are usually quoted as the main rationale for keeping utility companies in state ownership.

In the red mud case, the strong profit motive had two key effects. First, as has now been proven, MAL neglected to carry out the environmental remediation, whether prescribed in the privatization contracts or required by environmental regulations, such as the lowering of the pH levels of the sludge to nonhazardous levels, or the closure and recultivation of pond no. 10 by 2010. According to Zoltán Illés, the under secretary for environment, MAL was considering closing the alumina plant within the next few years, perhaps further encouraged in this plan by the economic crisis (*168 Óra* 2011). Illés cites the absence of any documentation that would indicate that MAL had been preparing to renew its environmental permit and switch to the dry technology.[14] He also suggests that after filling the ponds to their maximum capacity, which according to some had already been reached by the middle of 2010, they would have closed the plant, leaving debts and environmental damage behind. In a way this "get-rich-and-get-out-quick" scenario would have been an extended version of the partial privatization strategies mentioned above that sticks the taxpayers with the bills.

Second, circumstantial evidence suggests that MAL may have intended to turn the red mud impoundments themselves into profit-making units, which could have been done even after the closing of the plant. Two strategies came into play here: renting out lagoon space for other wastes, and future recovery of precious raw materials. Both projects have their own material conditions that go directly against remediation.

Red Mud as a Source of Profit

Lagoon Rental

Local residents I interviewed said they knew that MAL accepted other industrial waste for storage in the lagoons. They usually had no direct knowledge of this practice themselves, but quoted acquaintances that had worked at MAL. Such activity certainly would have required a host of environmental permits, and since the postdisaster investigations found no such documentation, MAL, if indeed it engaged in this practice, did so illegally. Therefore, getting people with firsthand knowledge of this to talk to me proved understandably impossible. There are two pieces of evidence that support the suggestion that MAL may indeed have "rented" out its disposal site to other companies. One comes from the chemical analysis of the spilled sludge. The international environmental organization Greenpeace's laboratory tests found chrome, mercury, and arsenic, compounds that should not have been there, or at least not in such concentrations, had the sludge only been composed of red mud; this is why the Hungarian Academy of Sciences team initially did not even think to look for them (Greenpeace 2010). Greenpeace had the tests performed by the Austrian Federal Environmental Protection Agency on samples collected on the fourth day after the disaster, and then had the results checked by a Hungarian private laboratory that receives commissions from the Hungarian Academy of Sciences itself, which should dispel any suspicions of the lab's bias in favor of Greenpeace. Eventually, more than two weeks after the catastrophe, the academy's own measurements basically confirmed Greenpeace's results (MTA 2010). The Greenpeace representative I interviewed interpreted these test results as evidence of illegal dumping of outside wastes.

The second piece of evidence comes from an almost cursory remark in the Parliamentary Committee's report. The document refers to a practice used in the already full and partially recultivated lagoons in Almásfüzitő, whereby hazardous wastes (from outside sources), mixed with organic wastes, were spread over their tops. The rationale for this procedure was that a relatively impervious layer had to be laid on top of the red mud before soil for plant covering could be spread on the surface, in order to prevent the salination of that soil.[15] According to the committee, however, a clay layer would have served this purpose sufficiently, implying that this was simply an excuse for using the ponds for disposing outside wastes. The committee went so far as to question the premise of composting hazardous byproducts by simply mixing them with organic wastes. It is possible that what some locals had interpreted as the dumping of outside wastes was in fact just such a practice.

Future Recovery of Precious Minerals

The profit motive, however, may have had yet another significant impact on the fate of the alumina waste. According to some informants, MAL had received offers from Russian and German companies to dredge up and rid the company of the sludge for free. Their interest was in recovering titanium and rare earth elements (REEs), currently among the most expensive raw materials in the world or subject to precipitous price rises due to environmental and political considerations.[16] This would have meant a big step toward local environmental remediation, because, as the technical literature on red mud disposal methods shows, the greatest difficulty in recultivating such impoundments comes from the need to move the massive volume of sludge safely. MAL, however, allegedly refused these offers because it hoped to recover those minerals itself in the future for its own gain. While right now the recuperation of aluminum, iron, titanium, and rare earth minerals is still very expensive, the burgeoning literature on recycling methods suggests that it might become economical in the future (Bánvölgyi and Huan n.d.; Binnemans et al. 2013; Kehagia 2008; Paramguru, Rath, and Misra 2005; Power, Gräfe, and Klauber 2009).

The technical literature—ever more optimistic about not just recuperating aluminum, titanium, and rare earth minerals from red mud, but also producing new products from it, such as bricks, ground cover, and fertilizer—seems to open up a different trajectory from that of the exhaustion of bauxite resources that, as mentioned, made many of the changes in the organization and ownership necessary: a trajectory not of disappearing but of newly appearing opportunities. While we have no proof that this is what M A L's owners indeed intended to do, or that they ever would have had the required technology and resources to realize a successful red mud recovery project, we have various pieces of circumstantial evidence that this scenario had been considered and even circulated among the interested parties. First, Szirmai's 1988 report already refers to the imperative of finding new uses for red mud, and as I have shown (Gille 2007), reuse enjoyed a high priority in state socialism—until the early 1980s, a higher one than safe disposal. Second, many of the authors of the international technical literature on reuse possibilities have been Hungarian (e.g. Bánvölgyi and Huan n.d.; Siklosi, Zoeldi, and Singhoffer 1991), and, given the smallness of the country, it is reasonable to assume that these academic experts and industry representatives formed an epistemic community (Haas 1992). In fact, Bakonyi himself had been in charge of Hungary's 1981 Waste and Secondary Raw Material Management Program, which had as its key goal to reduce waste and to find reuses for waste by technological innovation.[17] This makes it reasonable to conclude that he was well informed about the economic opportunities in recovering expensive materials from red mud and about the state of the waste management industry. Third, even the 2005 report of the National Development Agency (Nemzeti Fejlesztési Ügynökség) on the Ajka small region suggests that the "accumulated red mud could become the raw material for new [economic] activities" (National Development Agency 2005, 15).[18] In sum, the reuse and recycling of red mud had been talked about enough for these different reports to mention it as a rational and even expected future step.

The significance of this vision of mining the red mud ponds for economic gain resides in the technical synergies between the steps of remediation and mineral recovery. The technical literature suggests that the different recovery methods, on the one hand, and the dewatering and neutralizing of red mud, on the other, are parallel and intertwined processes. Two main methods have been tested for rescuing rare earth minerals from red mud (Binnemans et al. 2013). One is hydrometallurgical, the selective leaching of minor metals that leave behind the major metallic component, which, as mentioned, is iron oxide. The various elements then can be separated by the use of different solvents. The other method combines a hydrometallurgical with a pyrometallurgical process, which melts out the iron first and then proceeds to leach the sludge. Either method would be made even more complex and expensive if the red mud was first dewatered or otherwise neutralized, since the leaching requires both causticity and a liquid state. MAL, in sum, needed to postpone neutralization and remediation if it ever hoped to recover precious minerals in the future. The company's wait-and-see attitude that emerges from all the documents of the case—the fact that it didn't apply for an extension of the permit for the ponds and the fact that it didn't implement remediation—reflects this technological rationality.

THE EU'S REACTION

When the Hungarian public found out that red mud wasn't classified as hazardous waste—in contrast to the state socialist and postsocialist pre-accession periods—the initial shock was followed by many calls for re-classifying it. Among such voices were Hungarian members of Parliament from different parties and the Hungarian under secretary for environment, as well as the Romanian minister of environment and forestry, and Greens, including the Green Alliance of the European Parliament. Whether it was the EU or the Hungarian government that should implement this reclassification was initially unclear, however. Many were confused about whether the government could have retained the stricter classification or whether that would have gone against EU policy. Member states' governments in fact *can* categorize wastes as hazardous; they can always adopt a stricter classification than the EU's minimum. In addition, according to another criterion of EU waste policies, the Hungarian government not only *could* have but *should* have categorized it as such, because, according to its laws at the time of issuing the permit for pond no. 10 (in 2004), the pH was known to be higher than 9 and therefore "irritating" and "burning," which would automatically place Ajka's red mud in the hazardous category.

After understanding this possibility, more radical voices called on the EU itself to end the situation in which the classificatory ambiguity could result in a veritable deregulation of industrial wastes. In fact, Greenpeace, other environmental organizations, and the EUP's Green Alliance called not only for a reclassification of red mud as hazardous, but for closing loopholes in the EU's Mining Waste Directive, and for stronger enforcement, including establishing an EU-level capacity for environmental inspections. EU representatives, however, explained the disaster as a result of the negligence and incompetence of the Hungarian government. "We consider [that] they classified the red mud incorrectly in the original granting of the (environmental) permit. . . . It should have been classified as hazardous, it was classified as non-hazardous at the time," European Commission spokesman Joe Hennon said (*Earth Times* 2011). At the same time, officials emphasized that the Hungarian government was within its rights to classify red mud as nonhazardous and thus did not initiate punitive measures against the country. As Hennon clarified, "There may be no point in pursuing an infringement procedure: it depends on the systems the Hungarians have in place to grant permits . . . and what they plan to do on hazardous waste in general" (*Earth Times* 2011).

Commissioner Janez Potočnik described the information gathered from dialogue between the EU and Hungary this way:

> After the immediate crisis response phase, the Commission initiated a dialogue with the Hungarian authorities and requested information about implementation of the relevant pieces of EU environmental law. Questions were raised in particular with regard to the correct application of the Integrated Prevention and Pollution Control (IPPC) and Mining Waste Directives as well as the European Waste List.
>
> I have already mentioned our conclusion in the context of [the] Seveso Directive.
>
> The full application of the Directive on the management of extractive waste (2006/21/EC) to improve the safety of extractive waste facilities, including tailing ponds, would have been crucial in this case. Hungary did transpose the Directive on time, but it did not consider that this particular installation falls under its scope. We are now waiting for formal confirmation from the Hungarian authorities that the necessary changes in legislation have been carried out.
>
> We also found out that the waste in the red mud reservoir was classified as "non-hazardous," although according to the Commission, it should have been classified as "hazardous" due to the high alkalinity of the material. So we are now also waiting for formal confirmation that the new IPPC permit of the installation classifies the waste correctly, or that the technology used for the disposal of red mud is changed in a way that the hazardous properties of the waste are reduced.
>
> From what I have heard from the Under Secretary for Environment, Zoltán Illés, I am encouraged (Potočnik 2011).

EU representatives kept repeating that it was not the regulation but its implementation that was at fault. In response to questions as to why there had been no EU-level inspections in Ajka, Commissioner Potočnik responded to Greens' queries this way:

> I have been asked many times whether the red mud reservoir at Ajka was subject to the [Seveso] Directive. Let me clarify that the Directive normally applies to facilities of this sort provided that substances as defined under the Directive are present above set thresholds. Due to the specific substances and quantities involved, the Ajka site did not fall within its scope (Potočnik 2011).

The EU therefore not only deflected responsibility in this way but also justified its rejection of calls for reclassification or for a new mining waste policy.[19] In fact, the argument that the updating of the Seveso Directive was already under way took the wind out of the sails of any criticism regarding the EU's environmental laws.[20]

In fact, demands went in the opposite direction. After the disaster, experts and policy makers came to the conclusion relatively quickly that what was necessary was not reclassification or reregulation, but that MAL's technology conform to western European technology. The Hungarian state complied and assumed control over the company for the duration of this technological overhaul.

In 2011, MAL started switching to the dry technology by implementing three pressure filters that reduced liquid content to 50 percent (which makes the viscosity of red mud comparable to wet soil). But by 2012 the dry technology and the absence of plant covering produced the same problems it did under state socialism: the red mud dust was stirred up by winds and covered neighboring villages with a veritable wet cloud. The airborne dust particles once again—for the first time since the cleanup was complete in 2011—exceeded the legal maximum. In May 2012, the regional environmental authority (Közép-dunántúli Környezetvédelmi, Természetvédelmi és Vízügyi Felügyelőség) gave MAL a five-day deadline to end the source of the pollution, with which it could not comply, arguing that covering the lagoons is a very slow process due to the softness of the terrain over which machines necessary for this procedure have to move. In the end, the fines and continuous reorganizations that affected the company's ability to produce smoothly led in 2013 to MAL's bankruptcy. The

Hungarian government once again stepped in, this time more radically, to renationalize the company. The argument for nationalization was the strategic importance of alumina production and the continued employment of the people of the region (more than a thousand people, affecting, as they said, five thousand families' livelihoods).

THE TWO GAPS OF POSTACCESSION
ENVIRONMENTAL REGULATION

The best way to capture what path MAL and the Hungarian state had taken, which ultimately led to the disaster, is to adopt two anthropological notions of "gap."

One is Kevin Hetherington's (2004), which focuses specifically on waste practices. In his manifesto for a sociology of disposal—or, more narrowly, for the sociology of consumption to include waste—he argues that wastes are often not truly disposed of in the sense of settling the matter or the meaning of the discarded materials once and for all. If a thing is thrown away sooner than necessary, the prodigal discarding of value will come back to haunt us as loss or guilt. Alternatively, if we hold onto it too long, it will insinuate itself into our world with its smell and sight. In both cases, a badly managed absence unexpectedly becomes present. Hetherington suggests that such mismanagement is more common than we assume, and one way humans and collectivities have tried to avoid the consequences of such mismanagement is to accomplish disposal in two stages, known from anthropology as a first and a second burial. We need a gap—a transitional, liminal space if you will—where things can be held and denied the status of wastes, where some value might still be extracted from them.

Hetherington does not concern himself with industrial waste, and it is true that it is much more difficult for an industrial producer to create such gaps without violating existing environmental and public health regulations. Yet we can appreciate that, especially in conditions of economic uncertainty and poverty, a company may wish to postpone the final settlement of the discarded matter. In fact, that is exactly what studies focusing on the poor suggest when they describe their propensity to hoard potentially reusable or marketable scraps, rejects, and other consumer wastes. If the regulatory system is weak or in transition, as was the case with MAL, then the company will be able to adopt this gap strategy with impunity. Indeed, as mentioned above, throughout the parliamentary investigation MAL insisted that red mud is not waste but rather an intermediary material of alumina processing. Similarly, it wanted to avoid the classification of its ponds as disposal sites, using the argument that materials also leave the lagoons when some sodium hydroxide is recaptured and returned to the production process. Of course, categorizing the ponds as a "technological facility," rather than waste dumps, exempted them from disposal regulations, but it also kept a door open—using Hetherington's metaphor—to access the material for mineral recovery or other reuse technologies. Complying with disposal regulations and the privatization contract's stipulation that pond no. 10 should be closed by 2010 would have made any future access much more difficult, both from a technological and a legal-regulatory perspective.

The concept of gap is a simple aid in understanding how a postsocialist company in the midst of radical transformations in property structure, industrial restructuring, globalization, and regulatory reform tried to hedge its bets and played tag with the state, the game so many in those tumultuous years of the 1990s played. Understanding MAL's strategy and rational economic action is not the same as excusing its managers nor a call for exculpating them. But such an understanding that pays equal attention to materiality, temporality, and political economy, and to their interaction, could serve as a useful tool for fashioning environmental policy and waste regulation that fit local and non-Western realities better. To deepen this understanding, it is helpful to reach to another, broader anthropological concept of the gap, the one Anna Tsing (2005) sees as accompanying frictions.

When state socialism collapsed in eastern Europe, everybody conceptualized the tasks ahead of these countries in terms of time; there were hundred-day plans and five-hundred-day plans, not unlike the Five-Year Plans of centrally planned economies. There was supposed to be a chronology of milestones or benchmarks these countries would pass in a logical order. They for example could not become members of the European Union before democratic institutions were in place or before the market was judged to be operating freely enough. The 1993 Copenhagen Criteria put the conditions this way: "Membership requires that the candidate country has achieved stability of institutions guaranteeing democracy, the rule of law, human rights and respect for and protection of minorities, the existence of a functioning market economy as well as the capacity to cope with competitive pressure and market forces within the Union. Membership presupposes the candidate's ability to take on the obligations of membership including adherence to the aims of political, economic and monetary union" (European Commission 1993).

The absence of environmental harmonization suggests that marketization and democratization were seen as its prerequisites, and thus it could only follow after they were completed. An alternative order was said to be illogical. An example is the environmentalists' call for reining in the market via strict environmental regulation and the implementation of best practices in bidding, so that postsocialist countries could avoid the environmental problems the West had gone through. Instead, architects of the transition argued that first, everything has to be privatized, the old environmental policies have to be scrapped, and the state should get out of the economy. Once markets are free and the state cut back, then and only then, they said, can we start worrying about such luxuries as wastes and clean water. The way this order was manifest in the EU's accession politics was that political and legal institutions and a free market had to be in place prior to 2004, but environmental and particularly waste-related regulations received a derogatory period of ten to fifteen years.

But as the economy and the political regime went through momentous changes, the transformation took on an increasingly material character as well. Factories that once were the center of economic and social lives now stood in dilapidated ruins; public transportation thinned out and the car population exploded; banks and advertising billboards appeared on every corner, and post offices, daycare centers, and doctor's offices closed; old brands disappeared from the grocery stores, replaced by Western products that often didn't even have a label in the national language, leaving consumers at a loss as to what they were. Land- and cityscapes became glossier and more colorful *and* shabbier and grayer at the same time. A lot of things didn't fit, as evident from the pictures discussed in the introductory chapter. As new and old rubbed against each other, the object world came to look and function incongruously, and to get over such inconsistencies these societies developed gaps. Gaps were a kind of holding or bracketing that took up real space and had a real material nature.

As Tsing (2005) shows, friction often goes hand in hand with gaps. She calls gaps conceptual *and* real spaces "into which powerful demarcations do not travel well" (Tsing 2005, 175). In the red mud case, the gap resulted from the fact that legal harmonization, which always necessitates new material practices, can only take place in relatively small steps. While harmonization assumes a temporal progress, in practice it proceeds over space and materiality, and the so-called transitional periods are embodied in concrete—albeit incongruous—spatial and material arrangements.

Let me however make clear that there is a good reason not to refer to such instances as transition or a hybrid stage in which old and new still coexist, which will eventually "clear up" once the transition is complete. While any major social transformation will develop its own messiness and inchoateness, it would be a mistake to assume that such periods will always be superseded by a cleaner, neater, more logical, more coherent formation.[21] Nor can we assume that what is coherent is objectively definable; in fact, what from one perspective seems incongruent may indeed look like a mature case of this or that regime from another. Finally, we should not assume that a "clear case" of a social formation, for example of capitalism and liberal democracy, will necessarily be free of problems we see in transitions. We should not repeat the mistakes of formalist theories that can only notice those social problems that they see as resulting from some logical incoherence of the society in question or, vice versa, claim that all social problems are due to some logical incoherence of a society.[22]

Of particular importance in the red mud case are the circumstances: first, the postponement of the harmonization of waste policies, and second, the ignorance of the materiality of Hungarian alumina production. The derogatory period in the adoption of EU waste policies meant that many of Hungary's relatively strict regulations were suspended or continued to be relaxed—a trend that started in 1989—but without the enforcement of new policies. This created exactly the effect environmental experts had warned about, namely that producers would interpret it as an open season on nature and would see in them an endorsement if not an encouragement of illegal and unprofessional dumping and avoidance of material recovery and recycling. Knowing that in ten years their hands would be tied, businesses increased their imports of Western waste, and illegal dumping actually grew in the immediate aftermath of EU accession.

The murkiness of the policy environment was not simply a temporary blemish on the harmonization process. Treating environmental and waste issues as secondary to economic and market policies laid down a certain path of development, one that, after John Dryzek (1997), I call the "economic rationalism discourse." This is quite in contradiction to the EU's avowed path of ecological modernization, which sees economic development as synergistic with environmental protection. As I have argued elsewhere (Gille 2007), during this period a whole new infrastructure of end-of-pipe technologies—dumps and incinerators—was established, making preventive approaches, such as resource reduction and reuse, much less economical and depriving them of the necessary material conditions and financial resources. In sum, the "transitional" features got built into the now "coherent" and "clean" social formation. In such conditions, even if the Hungarian government had the correct understanding of its scope of authority in classifying red mud, in a discursive environment in which self-regulation of corporations was desirable and in which the EU's policies, including its waste classification, were a priori deemed better, it was unlikely that officials would have intervened. This larger context has never been acknowledged among the causes of the disaster. The following chapters will focus on the nature of this transnational and global context and its implications for the relationship between power and materiality.

NEOLIBERALISM, MOLECULARIZATION, AND THE SHIFT TO GOVERNANCE

T hroughout the case studies, as promised, I located myself at the global or transnational scale, but focused on what is concrete and particular. I ended up writing a lot about small, seemingly inconsequential things: paprika, fungi, geese, and industrial wastes. You are now justified in asking for the payoff. Why is it worth telling such little stories about little things from little villages in a little country? After all, the EU is a big thing, is it not? In the introduction I talked about smallness in two senses of the word. First is the sense of local and particular, where small refers to the size of a place, to its importance, or to its capacity to affect other places. The second meaning of smallness has been details or minor variations on something universal. One task left to do in this book is to reflect on the politics of connecting big and small things.

EUROPEAN UNION: SMALL OR BIG?

The question in the above title, to be sure, doesn't refer to the number of member states in this supranational organization. What I am asking is not whether to admit more countries into the EU or not, or whether previous waves of enlargement were right or successful. Rather I am asking a subtler, but not less consequential question: namely, what is the substance of the EU's coherence and power? My concern, to paraphrase Moss (2004), is not whether the EU works or should even exist, but *how* it works.[1] Such an inquiry, in turn, demands a much greater attention to the realm of "small things."

Over the past few decades, a number of intellectuals and politicians, including from the postsocialist region (Kundera 1984; Havel 1996), have lamented what one might call the bagatellization of the European Dream. Of course, different Europeans or EU citizens will dream of different things, but, written in capital letters, the "European Dream" refers to the official goal of a unified Europe: peaceful, affluent, but environmentally sustainable societies, governed by the rule of law, respectful of human rights, with a multiethnic, multireligious, and multicultural citizenry that is highly educated—thus governed by reason—and actively involved in public matters. What Václav Havel and Milan Kundera in particular, two influential Czech writers of the late twentieth century, the former also the first democratically elected president of his country after the collapse of state socialism, lamented was a seeming betrayal of the civilizational aspiration of the European Dream. Kundera had already in 1985 warned that Europe had given up on Culture with a capital C and was now reveling in consumerism. He argued that the only place where Culture still retained its—to use a Benjaminian phrase—auratic and thus politically emancipatory nature was Central Europe: Poland, Czechoslovakia, and Hungary. Havel, writing after 1989, objected to the EU's reduction of its mission to the micromanagement of the market and its ignorance of the role of European culture and identity—the latter admittedly aspirational—in fostering continent-wide integration. For his part, Manuel Barroso, president of the European Commission, in his 2013 State of the Union address, saw the relevance of this relationship between big and small in finding the right balance and scale of EU-level regulation. He stressed the importance of smart regulation and declared that the European Union "needs to be big on big things and smaller on small things" (Barroso 2013). Finally, political pundits have also connected "sweating the small stuff" to the EU's failure to stop the rise of the extreme right wing all over the continent—which ironically was a key raison d'être for a unified Europe in the first place.

I do not wish to join Kundera and Havel in regretting the decline of high culture in western Europe or the absence of cultural integration pursuant to Eurocentric Enlightenment ideals. Nor do I agree with Barroso and political pundits that the relationship between big and small is a zero-sum game, that if one pays too much attention to the latter, the former will suffer, and we will, to use another metaphor, miss the forest for the trees.[2] I do however want to call attention to the persistent presence of a particular politics of size in Europe, because such instances reveal certain aspects of the nature of power of this supranational entity, aspects I will fully elaborate in the next chapter. I will also show that this—the political attention to small versus big—is a much more structured and multidimensional relationship than the zero-sum assumption suggests. The remainder of this chapter will first lay down the foundation of a sociological approach to size and, second, look at how the scholarship on regulation—which after all is about connecting small with big things—would interpret these three case studies.

THE SOCIOLOGY OF SIZE

I am much inspired in this inquiry by Anna Tsing's (2009) and József Böröcz's (2010) rich explorations of how size has its politics and their invitation to social scientists to engage with size in more nuanced ways. Tsing (2009) encourages us primarily from a theoretical and epistemological perspective, asking how the implicit attribution of bigness to global capitalism influences how we characterize and go about studying globalization and capitalism.[3] She insists that we should not imagine bigness as homogeneity; in fact, she demonstrates through her study of Walmart that if supply chains are part of what makes global capitalism big, this bigness indeed relies on a particular heterogeneity and internal diversity. That we see it otherwise is simply evidence that we have bought the story capitalism tells about itself, which in turn is the story told about themselves by the most successful firms, who come to represent the right way of being big. She identifies three different ways of being big in three distinct epochs of global capitalism: GM's Fordist assembly line and its economies of scale; the franchise model of McDonald's that relies on the global distribution of standardized consumption and homogenous rules and regulations; and, finally, Walmart's supply chain model, dependent on its Voluntary Interindustry Commerce Standards (VICS), of which the Universal Product Code is the first and best known. Tying thousands of its suppliers to itself with a myriad of standards and codes is what allows this newest form of bigness to prevail. Here the relationship between homogeneity and diversity—which is Tsing's key interest, for the sake of understanding possibilities for political resistance—is not about either becoming more dominant, but of a different kind, in which a particular homogenization requires a particular type of diversification.[4]

Böröcz's (2010) concern with size resides less in defining bigness but is more closely related to my concern with the political nature of the European Union. In his 2010 book, he argues that the small size of western European nations has been, for the past five hundred years, a consistent obstacle to exerting the geopolitical influence that they thought should accrue to them based on their wealth. Key ways to overcome their insignificance—especially in terms of territory and population but often even in terms of their share of the world's economy—were colonization and, later, various strategies of regional integration, including the European Union. Innovations on the epistemological terrain, however, were also significant. A particularly successful method of convincing the world of these small countries' importance was a quantitative representation of their prowess Böröcz calls "ratist." This attitude is characterized by the statistical routine in which per capita indices—especially of wealth and GDP—are the sine qua non of all comparisons. Such metrics, he argues, are not innocent, but rather allow the hierarchical ordering of the world in which those with otherwise much greater territorial and population weight are regularly shown to be backward and thus in need of intervention, whether economic, military, or humanitarian. It is such "ratist" knowledge that in part justifies the development of contrasting political regimes in the metropole and the colonies: democracy and welfare for the former; authoritarianism, slavery, and neoliberalism for the latter.

My concern in this book has been with another aspect of size, one that could be seen as a synthesis of Tsing's and Böröcz's approaches. I am inspired by the relatively implicit focus of both authors on the practices by which the management of small things can yield big political and economic benefits. These practices, as many poststructuralist observers suggest, increasingly take place at the molecular level (Nally 2011; Rose 1999). Molecular here should not be taken literally, as it may also refer to supramolecular scales, such as genes and whole organisms, or to submolecular ones, such as atoms and some nanoparticles. Molecular rather is to evoke smallness. Rose's (1999) argument about what this smallness is and why it should be a focus of sociology and history goes like this:

> [S]o often in our history, events, however major their ramifications, occur at the level of the *molecular, the minor, the little, and the mundane.* So many of the texts which have later become canonical are retrospective attempts to codify such minor shifts. Yet events cannot be identified with these moments of formalization. Things happen through the lines of force that form when a multitude of *small shifts,* often contingent and independent from one another, get connected up: hence it is these *configurations of the minor* that seem to me to form the most appropriate object for the work of a historian of the present. (Rose 1999, 11, my emphasis)

Other times, what here appears a general epistemological and methodological program seems to be required because of ontological changes in the nature of government. Following Michel Foucault, Rose calls this new mode of power governmentality, which Foucault in turn saw as a specific historical development in nineteenth-century Europe:

> These links between the molar and the molecular have taken a variety of forms, not merely or principally paternalistic attempts at the micromanagement of conduct, but more complex and subtle procedures for establishing a delicate and complex web of affiliations between the thousands of habits of which human beings are composed—movements, gestures, combinations, associations, passions, satisfactions, exhaustions, aspirations, contemplations—and the wealth, tranquility, efficiency, economy, glory of the collective body. (Rose 1999, 6)

Both Rose and Böröcz make size a concern of power, though the former is more concerned with how power renders things small and thus relatively invisible, while the latter inquires into how states make something originally small big, more capacious in its impact. Furthermore, while Rose emphasizes that even in general and ontological terms molecular practices are contingent and incoherent, Böröcz tends to see planned, cohesive, and successfully executed strategies, whether material or epistemological. For Rose, all there are are vectors of change, which, while certainly ominous, do not necessarily express any particular power center's interests. Reading Böröcz, however, one almost senses a singular omnipresent and omnipotent actor. While I see my position somewhere between these two scholars', the thorny question of the agency behind connecting small with big things deserves a more nuanced exposition, especially because readers of the three cases will inevitably ask who orchestrated the paprika contamination, who funded the boycott of Hungarian foie gras, and who ignored the literal and metaphorical cracks on red mud containment. To start answering such questions of agency, let me suggest, and then reject, two possible interpretations of the case studies so that my own position can later be made clearer.

REGULATORY INTERPRETATIONS OF THE CASE STUDIES

Existing scholarship on regulation will likely see the paprika, the foie gras, and the red mud incidents as expressive of certain universal trends in regulation. I have already commented in the introduction on the dangers of seeing local stories as concrete variations of the general, but I do take these possible alternative interpretations seriously, because regulation, after all, is the art of connecting small with big things. For example, "big" ideologies or grand narratives, such as socialism or social democracy, cannot be put into practice without the mundane management of profits, taxes, wages, and welfare benefits, that is, regulation. Lest one thinks the opposing ideology, laissez-faire liberalism, requires no such state "interference," one must remember the history of Western capitalism, namely that the implementation of free markets to deliver the greatest good for the largest number of people also necessitated regulation. If nothing else, at the very basic level it required the state to regulate how private property can and should be protected, or how the "market-distorting" effects of oligopoly and monopoly—toward which all market economies show a natural tendency—should be curtailed. There is no need to rehearse these time-tested arguments; we just need to remember this basic feature of regulation as glue between big and small. I will mention two alternative interpretations: neoliberalism and the new regulatory paradigm of governance.

The Neoliberalism Argument

Some might interpret these cases as simply evidence of the triumph of neoliberalism; after all, looser regulation prevailed in all three of the cases.

To be sure, the EU continues not to require aflatoxin tests on imported spice peppers at EU customs borders, the EU hasn't banned the force-feeding of geese and ducks, and it certainly has not (re)classified red mud as hazardous waste. Appealing as this interpretation may be,[5] it ignores the context in which the cases occurred, which is that the European Union of the 2000s saw just as much regulation as deregulation. What's more, the very sectors and industries where these cases occurred themselves have been subjected to more and stricter regulation. The European Union has maintained or lowered its already strict maximum allowed concentrations of mycotoxins in fresh produce, nuts, and spices, and before, during, and after the Hungarian paprika scandal it continued to return to their original countries imported peppers—though not spice peppers—that tested positive for one or another contaminant. Standards concerning animal welfare in agriculture also increased; the most important legislation in the past ten years has been Council Directive 2007/43/EC on broiler chickens and Council Directive 2008/119/EC on calves.[6] Finally, the aluminum industry saw the implementation of new carbon trading and aluminum can recycling policies.[7]

Thus it is not so much that there has been an overall deregulatory turn, but that regulation was applied selectively. This raises the question of how it is decided—and by whom—which health, environmental, or animal rights concerns will be converted into more or stricter regulation. One circumstance that greatly influences such decisions is something the regulation and globalization scholarship has demonstrated unambiguously: the delegation of regulatory capacity to new, nonstate actors, and the transformation of the legal character of regulatory norms. It is this argument I turn to next.

The New Regulatory Paradigm Argument

Since the early 2000s, a new consensus has emerged in the social science scholarship on the relationship between globalization and regulation. In this view, globalization doesn't bring outright or universal deregulation, but rather a different mode of regulation. Here I will attend to four aspects of this shift: (1) the new actors doing the regulating, (2) the changing scale of regulatory actors, (3) the increasing voluntariness and "from-belowness" of regulation, and (4) the replacement of laws with standards and certificate schemes.

Some call this new mode "reregulation" or, better said, the strategic redistribution of issues over a more diverse field of regulatory oversight (Bartley 2014); others add that it is not so much the "amount" of regulation that has changed but the actors newly in charge of regulation, and its scale (Sassen 1995, 2000, 2006). Regulation, once the exclusive prerogative of the nation-state, is now "contracted out" to both subnational and supranational actors. Private actors, such as corporations, have been circumventing and preventing state regulation by implementing their own voluntary standards, whether in food safety, environment and health, or animal rights areas.

The trend has been so strong in environmental issues that European sociologists talked of a new era of modernity they called "ecological modernization." Proponents of ecological modernization theory see a transition in environmental discourse and practice primarily in the most developed countries, with the Netherlands and Japan leading the way (Hajer 1995; Mol 1995; Spaargaren and Mol 1992). They argue that although environmental protection previously tended to focus on how to "safely" displace hazards from production and concentrated on the distribution of hazards, now the intention is to keep and solve the problem of emissions and wastes within the sphere of production. It is in production that emissions can be reduced or prevented, and it is in production that byproducts can be reused or recycled. Such an internalization of environmental externalities is now seen as consistent with efforts to increase efficiency, and even as conducive to technological innovation. Furthermore, it has been argued that environmental impact may become decoupled from economic growth. In other words, changes in management and new innovations will lead to economic growth that no longer spurs commensurate increases in emissions or wastes.

Perhaps even more consequential than the novelty of the regulators' identity is the mode of regulation, which now increasingly takes the form of voluntary standards and certification schemes. Nongovernmental organizations, often arm-in-arm with corporations, design new codes of conduct and a whole slew of certification schemes. They span a variety of regulatory areas, but most important are the fields of environmental impact, for example the Forest Stewardship Council; EMAS (Eco-Management and Audit Scheme); food safety and hygiene, such as the aforementioned HACCP; and social aspects of production, for example Corporate Social Responsibility or Fair Trade, just to mention the best-known ones. Once these certificate schemes are designed, producers wishing to be certified make changes to certain aspects of their production—sourcing of raw materials, detection of potential contamination, remuneration of employees and suppliers—and subject themselves to an audit. Once successfully certified, they also commit themselves to regular routine monitoring, training, and other recertification procedures. In return, their products and promotional materials get to display the logo of the certificate in question, which then transfers onto them all the economic benefits associated with branding.

The social sciences didn't miss this trend and produced a number of sociological and anthropological studies of standards that are also theoretically sophisticated (Appelbaum, Felstiner, and Gessner 2001; Vogel and Kagan 2004; Garsten and Jacobsson 2011; Busch 2000, 2004; Bingen and Busch 2006; Gereffi, Garcia-Johnson, and Sasser 2001; Freidberg 2004; Brunsson et al. 2000; Dunn 2003, 2004, 2005, 2007).[8]

Without promising comprehensiveness, let me summarize these authors' main arguments. First, most of them agree that there has been a growing trend in the creation of standards, which in turn facilitates globalization in that it makes economic cooperation, the transnational extension of commodity chains, and trade smoother by reducing transaction costs. Second, however, most observers also admit that other costs—besides transaction costs—especially those incurred at the initial adoption of these standards, are quite high, and, depending on the sector, the periodic monitoring and auditing expenses can also be substantial. Standardization thus tends to favor the largest suppliers, something the European Union's own studies now explicitly admit (Arete n.d.; London Economics 2008), and the United Nations' various organizations have also flagged as an issue to tackle (Brown 2005; Brown and Sander 2007).[9] In a third key focus of the literature, scholars have also questioned the effectiveness of the standards in achieving the promised results, whether lower environmental impact, fairer treatment of direct producers, or treating farm animals more humanely (OECD 2003). Here a shared finding has been that local conditions are often inhospitable to standards (Juntti 2012; Lampland and Star 2009), or that there is a lot of work and tweaking necessary on the ground for the standards to be implemented. Fourth, of particular question, though there has been less attention to this issue, is whether the standard in question elevates norms above existing regulatory requirements, legitimates already existing actual practices, or lowers norms below them toward a minimum threshold that all designers and adopters of the standard can agree on. Fifth, the expertise involved and the slate of participants in designing standards has also been critically examined, highlighting the economic disadvantage that results from excluding certain actors and certain types of knowledge from the design and implementation process.

Perhaps the question animating most social scientists, especially those thinking about standards the most theoretically, is the relationship between democracy and standards. Most have agreed, quite independently from the economic sector or area of regulation for which they were designed, that unlike regulation designed and mandated by democratically elected parliaments and governments, standards are usually developed in less transparent fora. These tend to be inhabited by individual firms, industry associations, NGOs, or multistakeholder initiatives (MSIs), a group of people, usually representatives of different institutions, identified as having an interest in the outcome of a decision, in this case the design of a regulatory standard (Hatanaka and Konefal 2013).[10] On balance, the emerging consensus on standards is more negative than positive, with the two key conclusions that governing through standards infringes upon democracy,[11] and, as Timmermans and Epstein (2010) claim, that standards are not just "soft regulation," but, due to their market rearranging and exclusionary effects, are also a "soft form of stratification" (84).

In light of the literature on standards, my case studies could easily be seen as exhibiting the above-mentioned negative social consequences of standardization: the use of standards for protectionist or expansionist economic goals, the exclusion of a particular set of "stakeholders" from the design and application process, and the resulting exclusion and economic marginalization of affected producers. I must admit that for a while this was my interpretation as well. However, a few facts don't fit. First, the proliferation of standards doesn't explain the red mud case. After all, in that instance no private standards applied in this industry, and the disaster had more to do with the interpretation of supranational and national regulation. Second, while the paprika and foie gras stories might appear as case studies of the implementation of food safety and animal welfare standards, the foie gras boycott, as I have argued, hasn't actually resulted in nor was it the result of private or civic standards or certification schemes. And while some social scientists do call attention to the blurry boundary between formal and informal standards (Lampland and Star 2009), the difference is significant, not just from an analytical point of view but also for producers' economic situation. Even in the paprika case, where after all there had been a prior implementation of food safety standards, most notably HACCP, the standard was not required by private entities, but rather by the European Union as a condition of accession, and the effect of the standard cannot be simply demonstrating a race-to-the-bottom nor a race-to-the-top effect. This is because it was adopted in a particular transnational matrix, including the EU customs union and selective testing at EU customs borders, which in turn reflected the largest and most influential economic interests in western Europe.

This has two implications for the scholarship on standards. First, in order to understand the above-mentioned undemocratic and stratifying effects of standards or quasi-standards (such as the ban on foie gras production in most EU member countries), more attention needs to be paid to the synergy or complex relationship between state actors and private labels. Second, the mechanisms by which standards contribute to transparency, democracy, or fairness and the actual protection of consumers, farm animals, or small producers will greatly depend on the transnational economic and political context in which the standards operate. To understand how standards do what they do and with what consequences, in cases where they not only "travel" from more powerful to less powerful nations and economic actors but are also mandated by supranational actors, lessons learned from globalization and neoliberalism must be added to our explanatory repertoire.

With such provisos on standardization as the key explanatory factor of the case studies, and a signal that in the last section of this chapter I will come back to one significant, albeit much ignored, function of standards, we are now ready to move on to a final argument in the new policy paradigm interpretation.

Pointing to the slew of new private and civil society actors who now routinely undertake several of the regulatory tasks of the nation-state, many scholars have identified a shift from government to governance. The latter refers to a type of regulation that is more nimble because it can be more responsive to specific and rapidly changing needs than the blanket policies of national governments, which require "slow" legislative decisions and are deemed too general to be effective. Thus governance-type regulation reflects the needs of a new capitalism many have named flexible accumulation.[12] In this new regime of accumulation, the faster, leaner, more nimble, and flatter corporations will have the advantage, and governments must accommodate this new way of doing business.

In addition to corporations and nongovernmental organizations that are multinational, there are also other new regulatory actors at the supranational scale. Scholars have paid the most attention to those that have taken over more and more of the fiscal, trade, and economic policy decisions of nation-states, such as the International Monetary Fund (IMF), the World Bank, and the World Trade Organization (WTO), but the United Nations and the European Union have also been studied from this perspective. A shared finding is that as the nation-state deregulated or at least cut back on its "interference" in the economy and society, these supranational agents replaced national-level regulation with their own codes, norms, and rules. It is fair to say that the goals of some of this top-down policy making were achieved. After all, they did foment trade, reduce transaction costs of business deals, and prevent allegedly market-distorting government action. What has been less recognized by these supranational actors, however, is an overall negative effect on democracy. First, it is important to remember that to the extent that officials and policy makers in these organizations are appointed rather than elected, they are less accountable to the citizenry of the nations that are members of these organizations. Second, in the name of freer trade, many regulations previously put on the books by democratically elected legislators and governments—often preceded by decades-long social movements—were eliminated; this too can be seen as undermining democratic rule making.

Related to the above-detailed change in the cast and scale of regulation is another trend scholars have called attention to: the increasing "reflexivity" of policy making. Usually what they mean by this is the willingness of policy makers to include the public in designing new standards and rules (Paul 2012; Gereffi, Garcia-Johnson, and Sasser 2001). Many developed countries and some supranational organizations, such as the U N and the EU, now require "consultation" with nongovernmental actors prior to new legislation that affects their membership or the causes for which they work.[13]

Those who see increasing reflexivity in policy making might argue that the foie gras case in particular testifies to a welcome involvement of a nongovernmental organization in jump-starting a campaign for stricter standards in the treatment of farm animals. They, however, miss a number of facts. First, reflexivity doesn't automatically mean greater accountability. In fact, the participation of nonelected actors, such as the Austrian animal rights organization, in policy making might reduce accountability; after all, they cannot be recalled should the public disagree with them. Second, the involvement of the public in deliberations about policy so far has failed to be truly transnational; while there may have been public discussion and perhaps even agreement in one country on a particular issue, that doesn't mean that the public in another country has been heard. You may find, hypothetically speaking, that the Dutch public has had a chance to deliberate and shape policy concerning the force-feeding of geese, or you may find that the Spanish Chamber of Commerce endorses the absence of aflatoxin testing of spice peppers, for example, but that doesn't mean that legislation generated by such "reflexive" and "deliberative" procedures will indeed be reflexive and legitimate in Hungary, where there has been no comparable discussion. The foie gras and paprika cases therefore are, at best, examples of selective and uneven implementation of the reflexive policy-making paradigm, which results not in greater reflexivity but in preserving existing inequality between western and eastern Europe.

The Cultural Commodification Argument

There is one last function of standards that I have not paid attention to, and that is that even if the adoption of a standard doesn't yield the kind of benefits it promises—environmental improvement, quality control, hygiene, etc.—the mere seal of approval of a particular standard will give that business a coveted image that can be converted into high added value for one's product. We may say that standards function as brands. This signifying value of standards, to borrow Baudrillard's term, is particularly important in increasing the confidence of businesses or investors in new entrants to the world market, such as those from eastern European postsocialist countries. This ancillary function—but according to Storz (2007) occasionally the main reason for the adoption of standards in some cases—closely resembles the effect of a new trend diagnosed and analyzed by Jean and John Comaroff (2009).

In *Ethnicity, Inc.,* the Comaroffs identify a new relationship developing among culture, ethnicity, and the market, or to be more precise, the commodity form. There is a new identity economy, in which ethnicity is the key economic resource, so that not only are cultural practices and products commodified (produced for the market), but ethnicity itself is also increasingly rendered in a corporate form. Correcting earlier, mostly Marxisant, analyses of commodification, however, the Comaroffs argue that in these new "ethnopreneurial" (meaning not only ethnicized but also self-commodifying) activities, the market and culture are no longer antithetical, and, contra Benjamin and Adorno, the reproduction of culture doesn't eliminate authenticity or the aura of folk art, nor does it prevent political consciousness. Instead, there is evidence that it is this commodification that produces ethnicity, even fashioning it out of whole cloth where previously it did not exist. A good example is Bafokeng Inc., which—in order to reap the economic benefits of titanium mining on their territory, a Tswana nation in South Africa—incorporated and thus created the identity of the San people. The San had previously been fragmented, had practiced precious few, if any, of the rituals regularly enacted after incorporation, and had felt, at most, a residual sense of shared belonging. Relevant for all cases like this is the rendering of "ethnic" groups as legal persona, which seems the most winning strategy in accessing hotly contested economic resources in the age of neoliberalism.

Indeed, there are many other legal tools serving similar purposes that the Comaroffs could have included in their book. Various intangible heritage protection projects, primarily the operation of the UN's World Heritage List (Farmer 2014; DeSoucey 2010); the creation of traditional knowledge databases (TKDs) (Chander and Sunder 2004); communal rights and intellectual property in indigenous species of plants or other patentable life forms; and geographic indicators (GIs) are the most widespread legal instruments. While these accomplish very different things for different purposes and by different actors, they are all projects of standardization, whose goal is to fix the essence and the boundaries of a cultural product or life form developed in a particular cultural context, in order to conserve it. This conservation, however, is not aiming at museumification—sparing the object in question from use—but rather at increasing its consumption, albeit within strict guidelines. The territory, the method of production, and the ingredients are the most common limitations. Nevertheless, it is fair to say that the logic of this type of conservation is that the more such protected products can be consumed, the more likely they will be conserved and shielded from unfair competition.

Social scientists have pointed out many undesirable consequences of such cultural commodification schemes, most of which derive from standardization. Fixing the genome of a pig worthy of the heritage species designation goes against naturally occurring mixing and thus biodiversity (Lotti 2010). Drawing the boundaries of a *terroir* is often arbitrary, with the result that certain manufacturers of the same good are prevented from enjoying the GI designation and all its associated economic benefits (Farmer 2014; Lotti 2010), often in a way that benefits those who had the resources to initiate the GI approval to begin with. This in turn excludes potential variations from the cultural product, an effect that contradicts the spirit of conserving cultural diversity. These are just some of the negative environmental and social consequences, and, to be sure, they do not necessarily occur in all cases. What is more important to keep in mind is the similarity of the logic and outcomes of voluntary standards, discussed in the previous section, and these commodified cultural objects.

Some of these similarities are due to the shared context in which both safety, quality, and environmental standards, on the one hand, and ethnocultural commodification, on the other, occur. The Comaroffs explicitly trace this trend to the rise and spread of neoliberalism, which, in many countries of the Global South especially, creates a situation in which the state can make less and less of a pretense of protecting the land, the economic opportunities, and the autonomy of various, mostly minority groups. This leaves them with little else to do but to turn the only remaining "thing" they have left—their culture and their identity—into a marketable resource.

It is necessary to include this trend because even though cultural commodification, in all its variety of legal instruments listed above, is not a policy paradigm per se, it provides an important context for the change in the nature of politics in the European Union I will identify in the conclusion. Indeed there have been signs of people catching onto this new use of culture after Hungary joined the European Union. Evidence for this comes in part from the satirical poster exhibition, organized annually in Hungary, called *ArcPlakát*. A few of these posters can be seen in the figures that follow.

All three posters deliver the primary message that one way to retain Hungarianness is to package it in a Euro-conforming—an appealing, luxurious, or appetizing—way. Paprika can be our way to the West—here represented by the "alohawillkommen" hybrid greeting—if we take it out of its original milieu and field of use and hang it as a necklace on a sexy nude. The image of garlic wrapped as precious chocolates also suggests that our success in the EU depends on the correct "packaging" of our cultural or culinary possessions, no matter how mundane and seemingly

"Alohawillkommen." By Katalin Baráth and Gameman, 2006.

"Sztereotípia" (Stereotype). By Borbála Koppándi, 2006.

"Eudoboz" (EU box). By Rudolf Halmai and István Rózsa, 2005.

worthless. The third poster makes the message even more explicit by calling the box that contains so many Hungarian feature products and brands, such as the Rubik's cube, Franz Liszt, paprika, and Tokaj wine, the "EU expansion kit."

Resonating with this idea of "correct packaging" is the interpretation of Europeanization as civilization, in the sense of a process. Many, especially on the Euro-skeptic end of the political spectrum, have expressed suspicion about the *civilizing* mission of the European Union and objected to the tutorial role the West played vis-à-vis Hungary. Others, for example the creators of the Romanian slideshow introduced at the beginning of this book, welcomed this civilizing mission. To be sure, the idea that eastern Europe is in need of such outside assistance is not an entirely indigenous view. Centuries of historiography described this part of Europe as a deficient copy of the West, whether in terms of economic development, democracy, or the culturedness of its people (in the French sense of *civilité* or in the German sense of *Bildung*).[14] Communist ideologues themselves always talked about the need to catch up with the West, and after the collapse of their regime, the European Union and an army of Western experts tutored eastern Europeans on how to progress and improve themselves, whether as managers, employees, NGO activists, elected officials, consumers, or women.[15] A visual, though satirical, representation of a more critical view of this civilizational mission can be seen on the poster "Evolúció" submitted to the aforementioned *ArcPlakát* exhibitions.

Let us notice a deeper, and probably not conscious, message of these posters, as well as of those sampled from in the introduction. West and East appear, in the words of Holland et al. (1998), as "figured worlds."[16] Civilization is far from being a purely ideational process; rather, the materiality in which West and East appear and with which they are associated (though not in a way that is free of stereotypes and misconceptions) comes to form an integral part of people's self-conception, so that identity projects cannot help but be expressed in or accompanied by projects to change the object world. While buildings, public spaces, and monuments heavy with political symbolism have always been impacted by political changes, especially in the wake of changes as momentous as the collapse of state socialism in Europe, today a larger pool of objects are impacted: clothing, food and meals, homes, shop fronts, even bodies. This is because, as Tim Dant (2006) argues, the *habitus* of the late modern individual is more than ever constituted by or dependent on material things. This makes it necessary, in his mind, to understand today's culture not purely in symbolic but also in material terms. To capture the material aspect of culture, he suggests the concept of material civilization.

"Evolúció" (Evolution). By László Róbert, 2005.

To summarize, if we understand the EU as a particular object world and its civilizational impact as transforming not simply east Europeans' hearts and minds, but also their materiality and everyday practices, the *Ethnicity, Inc.* paradigm emerges as wanting. It misses the crucial tool that makes cultural commodification possible, namely the material—and not just cultural—standardization of culture and identity. This, in turn, is important for understanding the types of political questions I have grappled with in this book. Just as Mukerji has made the concept of figured world evolve to a "figured world of power," I too must explore the actual practices of power that result in phenomena such as *Ethnicity, Inc.* describes. None of the two—or three including the Comaroffs—regulatory interpretations described above fully explain how and why we had what I characterized in the introduction as triboelectric effects (explosions) because, as I will show, they miss a more fundamental shift in connecting big and small things, a shift that underlies all three. What if the reason culture, identity, and the market are now unpredictably intertwined is because there is a new political substrate that underpins their connection? What if the reason reflexivity and public involvement is now accepted and even expected in EU practice is because some of the most consequential policy interventions are no longer made in the open court of parliamentary democracy, but in the less transparent realm of nonhuman actors? It is this new political modality I will turn to.

CONCLUSION

THE MATERIALIZATION
OF POLITICS

The three case studies examined here attest to a new way of connecting small and big things, achieving political ends with seemingly apolitical material tools. To understand this relationship between materiality and politics, it is helpful to return to the images that opened this book. The iconographic self-representations of the European Union and the common visual symbols of globalization express a certain belief in a particular type of progress. In their promise of a freedom from place and matter we see the modernist utopia identified by Bruno Latour (1993a). In *We Have Never Been Modern*, he demonstrates that the separation of the social from the natural sciences was neither natural nor an automatic development, but rather rested on the claim that society and nature are distinct and independent from one another. This, in turn, was proposed by and became the hegemonic assumption in Western societies with the Enlightenment. The presumption of such a separation was necessary to sustain the belief that as societies progress, humans will master nature and mold the nonhuman world to their needs. Latour instead insists that, not unlike our premodern ancestors, we too still live in a hybrid —both a social and material—world.

As a minor corrective to Latour, we must admit that such a dream is not the exclusive property of the Enlightenment, but of most world religions as well. From Christianity to Buddhism, there is an encouragement of a denial of, or at least a detachment from, the grittiness of our bodies, from the miserable conditions our natural environment can expose us to, and from the objects we love to have around us—from libations to comfy chairs to fashionable clothes. Yet as Daniel Miller (2002) points out, all these religions prescribe specific practices and particular material conditions in order to achieve such exalted transcendence of materiality. You may need to sit in a specific pose, breathe in a specific way and in relative silence in order to meditate, to eat or refrain from certain foods, to wear certain things, or to prostrate yourself in particular directions. The desired spiritual effects in which we can expect to transcend our physical surroundings and body require practices that are material and embodied.

It is no less so with globalization or the European Union. Indeed, many scholars advocate what we might call a grounded view of globalization, a perspective of transnational social relations that sees local materialities as not only consequential but necessary for a particular version of globalization or Europeanization to succeed. This body of scholarship arose in opposition to claims that the social, under conditions of globalization, is characterized by an all-encompassing fluidity, connectivity, or borderlessness, such as Manuel Castells' (1989, 1997) concept of network society; Arjun Appadurai's (1990) suffix-like concept of scapes; John Urry's (2000) view that mobilities make the very concept of the social passé; or David Harvey's (1990) argument that there is a universal time-space compression. Against these scholars, Saskia Sassen (1995, 2000) has argued that fluidities rely on fixities and that the state is still a key anchor and facilitator of capital and labor mobility; Anna Tsing (2000) has shown that in order for things to flow, channels have to be built; and Jan Nederveen Pieterse (2002) has claimed that borderlessness comes at the expense of erecting new borders. Arguments such as these echo claims that globalization, flexible accumulation, and neoliberalism are not automatic or natural processes, but strategic projects by particular actors (McMichael 1996; Hart 2002; Evans 1997; Burawoy et al. 2000).

Arriving at the same claim about the enduring, if not increasing, significance of the concrete, of the local, and the material is another area of scholarship or, more precisely, a few loosely related theoretical approaches converging in what is called the practice or material turn. Certainly there is reliance in this turn on older social science traditions, such as Marxism, second-wave feminism, Peircian material symbolism, material culture studies (and even earlier folklore studies), science and technology studies, and Bourdieuian sociology. While I cannot carry out an involved analysis of the relationships and differences among these traditions, it is necessary to signal two important directions in the new scholarly attention to materiality so I can highlight my contribution to this scholarship in as clear a way as possible.[1] One is the elevation of the social scale at which nonhuman actors participate in constituting the purely social or purely cultural, which I include under the subheading transnational hybrid ontologies; the other is a more consistent attention to the relationship between materiality and power.

TRANSNATIONAL HYBRID ONTOLOGIES

What does materiality mean? It does not mean materialism, and certainly theoretical traditions that see society as hybrid—composed of humans and nonhumans equally—are not necessarily materialist.[2] By materiality, I refer rather to the physical world that surrounds us: nature, manmade objects, our bodies, and, even more broadly, the way space is organized around us and the concrete practices and technologies we employ in our everyday life. While after the practice and material turns we no longer hold the assumption that the nature of this materiality is, well, immaterial, there has been little exploration of the question of at what social or geographical scale the object world and nature matter. This is because of the widespread conflation of social scale with level of abstraction. It has been assumed that the concrete, the particular, and thus the material always operate at the micro-social level or in the local. Fernand Braudel, who explored precisely the relationship among different social scales in the world-system, was not free of this assumption himself. In his magnum opus *The Structures of Everyday Life* (1981), he presents social reality between the fifteenth and eighteenth centuries as a tripartite structure: (1) the uppermost sphere of wealth concentration and foreign exchange, (2) the market economy, this most familiar sphere of production and exchange in its most visible forms (small shops, banks, markets), and below all this, (3) the zone of material life, "the world of self-sufficiency and barter of goods and services within a very small radius" (Braudel 1981, 24), the sphere where transformation was the slowest, but on which the upper two layers depended. Braudel of course does not use language characteristic of actor-network theory, such as nonhuman agency, but his actual case studies focusing on specific material, biological objects and processes nevertheless demonstrate that each age has its limits and possibilities determined by this "shadowy" zone of everyday practices. Braudel also does not draw the conclusion, implicit in some environmental history (see below), that precapitalist and capitalist social relations gained their key features from the materiality of the means and conditions of production. Rather this micro level is presented as the particular of the universal macro, as local(ized) and static, especially in relation to the networked, transnational (24), and dynamic upper zone. For him, too, materiality is to be captured at the local or micro level, and this micro level is occupied by "place," conceptualized as in stasis.

Sidney Mintz (1986) was much inspired by Braudel and the Annales School, and his classic study demonstrates the role sugar—or, as he prefers to designate the object under investigation, "sweetness"—played in the formation not just of the colonial empires but also of capitalism in Europe. He pays particular attention to the material qualities of sugar cane, such as its "need" for speedy harvesting and processing and the difficulty of smuggling it in its preprocessed form, which made it a good tax commodity, as well as its ability to provide a quick infusion of a large dose of calories into the human body, a quality which made it an ideal "fast food" for the growing industrial working class newly subjected to machine time. Here the materiality of sugar played an important role in facilitating the circulation of people and capital, which helped it maintain European empires.[3]

Timothy Mitchell's (2002) work on the role of science, statistics, maps, and nonhuman agents, like mosquitoes and paper, in colonizing and modernizing Egypt is in many respects a continuation of the kind of historiography developed by Braudel and Mintz, but it owes more to Latour. In *Rule of Experts*, Mitchell demonstrates how nonhuman agents were enrolled in the colonizing project, but also how some of them produced distinct economic and political outcomes quite independent of and often contradictory to a modernizing, capitalist, or colonialist logic. It must be remembered that while ultimately proposing a correction to it, Braudel, Mintz, and Mitchell all constructively engage with Marxism.[4] They all see capitalism as a worldwide or close to global formation, and their work on the role of nonhumans in not just making possible but shaping the nature of connections across the globe has much inspired my inquiry into the material conditions of the European Union.

Environmental historians have long been trailblazers of incorporating nature's and materials' agency into our understanding of seemingly purely social transformations, and Donald Worster's *Dust Bowl* (1979) and William Cronon's *Nature's Metropolis* (1991), major interventions into that field, provided another encouragement for my investigation of how nature or materiality travel at a global scale. Worster demonstrates how the insertion of European species and modes of cultivating the land into an unfit landscape contributed to the "natural" disasters called dust bowls in the prairies of North America in the 1920s and 1930s. Cronon's work, an environmental history of Chicago, explodes the city-country divide to illuminate urban-rural interdependence, a purpose, according to him, best served by a variety of stories about the paths that lead from Chicago to its hinterland. He describes how nature (geography, climate, and natural resources), taken for granted as the ecological condition of Chicago's birth and development, was in fact a construction informed by the social interests of Chicago's boosters and other social actors. He implies that their concepts of ecological givens were not endogenous to the society in which they lived, but were derived from knowledges of different kinds of environments. Here too we see the effort to get away from deriving the spatial and ecological changes of the emergent Chicago from an overall logic of capitalism, as is evident in Cronon's refusal to trace concrete historical processes to any kind of metalogic of capitalist growth, urbanization, or the conquering of the frontiers. *Dust Bowl* and *Nature's Metropolis* can also be seen as studies of frictions resulting from the imposition of European materiality—species, agricultural practices, transportation technologies, and other practices—on the landscape of the American Midwest.

Moving to a more self-conscious and programmatic investigation of materiality at the supralocal and supranational scales is actor-network theory (ANT), even though it does not wish to endorse any scalar distinctions. Latour, the "founding father" of ANT, hypothesizes a hybrid ontology in which humans and nonhumans constantly cocreate each other, hence the talk of "actants" rather than actors. Latour uses the metaphor of network to decenter human agency. While in recent iterations of ANT, Latour (2005) and John Law (2007), another scholar associated with ANT, have both reflected self-critically on the network metaphor—and lately Latour tends to talk about sociomaterial assemblages—this concept has been foundational and consequential for their empirical studies and the further elaboration of their theoretical arguments against traditional social science. The best empirical demonstration of the concept's utility, especially on a global scale, is Latour's *The Pasteurization of France*. In it, Latour (1993b) rewrites the story of Pasteur's role in developing modern medical science. He *decenters* the human actor, Pasteur himself, by demonstrating how it was not Pasteur but the network he built of doctors, hygienists, bacteria, farms, animals, state bureaucrats, laboratories, and colonial authorities that instigated the progress usually credited to the sole scientist. At the same time, he also *recenters* Pasteur and his network in the sense that he argues that what Pasteur's web reformed was not only medical practice but society itself. By institutionalizing new scientific knowledge, practices in a whole slew of arenas of social life radically changed, and these practices also shifted the balance of power by empowering some actors (doctors, the colonial army) while disempowering others (indigenous Africans). In fact, these social actors were no longer identical with their pre-Pasteur selves. France as a colonial power, for example, no longer consisted only of settlers, the church, a colonial bureaucracy, and an occupying army, but also of bacteriological science and practices such as laboratory tests and immunization. In short, this view of France is not one of classes, parties, ethnicities, or institutions, but of a network, in which nodes can be nonhuman as well as human.

The model of entangling the social with the material that engages with globalization studies and multiple scales the most self-consciously is provided by the volume *Global Assemblages*, edited by Aihwa Ong and Stephen Collier (2005). Like Mitchell, the contributors follow ANT, poststructuralism, convention theory, and other primarily European contemporary theories of late capitalism and neoliberal governmentality. The case studies examine specific phenomena—"technoscience, circuits of licit and illicit exchange, systems of administration or governance, and regimes of ethics or values" (Ong and Collier 2005, 4)—that articulate the kinds of shifts previously only captured at the global scale by universal concepts. Ong and Collier's concept of assemblage, taken from ANT, is the product of multiple determinations that are not reducible to a single logic;

assemblage refers to the level of the concrete. They also emphasize that the temporality of the assemblage is emergent. "It does not always involve new forms, but forms that are shifting, in formation or at stake" (Ong and Collier 2005, 12). Some of the authors in this rich volume rely on Andrew Barry's (2001) concept of the technological zone, "a space of circulation within which technologies take more or less standardized forms" (Barry 2001, 122). This too is a fluid concept. These are spaces formed when technical devices, practices, artifacts, and experimental materials are made more or less comparable and connectable, but they are not fixed structures; "they demand regeneration, adjustment, and reconfiguration: frequent maintenance work" (Barry 2001, 40). Barry acknowledges that Europe as a technological zone is not smooth and perfectly well connected, where capital and labor circulate without impediments, but argues that they are full of "fractures and discontinuities." Yet the concept does refer to comparability and connectability, and thus in my mind to compatibility; and as such it does not make space for from-below constructions of alternative compatibilities or even the lack of compatibility. For this reason, the types of friction analyzed in this book would fall outside its purview.

In general, neither the concept of global assemblages nor that of technological zones recognizes that micro or macro logics are qualitatively different, and as a result they ignore the relative autonomy of the macro or the global scales. This is understandable given that both major theoretical inspirations for the volume (as well as for Barry's work), ANT and poststructuralism, hope to transcend the micro-macro divide. There are good methodological and theoretical reasons for retaining this distinction, and there is a political reason as well.

POLITICS AND MATERIALITY

Philosophers, historians, and social scientists have demonstrated that agents of power have often been able to rely not simply on sheer violence or nonphysical tools of domination such as laws, other social institutions, or culture, but also on a particular arrangement and use of objects, landscapes, animals, spaces, and bodies.

Perhaps the earliest general formulation of this relationship between materiality and power came from the representatives of the Frankfurt

School, and from Herbert Marcuse (1964) in particular. Relying on Weber, Marx, and Freud, he demonstrated how in late capitalism (for him the United States of the 1950s and 1960s), domination over humans is increasingly embedded in the technologically rational organization of production and consumption. Foucault (1977, 2003, 2010) continued this theme of management qua domination in his analyses of concrete institutions of modernity, such as the asylum, schools, hospitals, and prisons. Both argued that these techniques of power are more efficient, seemingly less tangible, and more impersonal, thus making it more difficult for people to see through and resist them. Underlying both Critical Theory and Foucauldian thought is the premise that social actors can indeed design and control technologies and spaces in a way that best serves their interests and that the materiality they bring into existence will indeed produce the intended effects on people, whether acquiescence, obedience, discipline, or productivity.

Langdon Winner (1986), in his path-breaking work on the relationship between technology and democracy, has argued that sometimes a certain technology is explicitly implemented in the interest of producing certain, often antidemocratic, political effects; other times, negative political outcomes are merely "unintended consequences." An example of the former is David Noble's (1984) study of technological innovation in industry, which he found often to be motivated by managers' need to decrease workers' control over the production process—which would weaken the power of labor unions—rather than by a short-term interest in increasing efficiency and profitability. More recently, Timothy Mitchell (2009) argues that the shift from coal to oil as a main source of energy in postwar Europe, encouraged and subsidized by the United States, was similarly aimed at breaking the power of coal workers and socialists. An example of the latter—of unintended political consequences—comes from the historian Karl Wittfogel, cited and expanded on by environmental historian Donald Worster (1985), who shows that hydraulic societies, such as ancient Egypt and twentieth-century California, are heavily dependent on tapping into and then distributing scarce water resources. Since irrigation channels require major planning and coordination, these societies all tend to develop highly centralized and stratified structures. That is, in order for rivers to flow where water is needed, social power must flow upward to install and operate the complex materiality of irrigation. A similar centralizing and even despotizing effect has been attributed to nuclear power plants (Winner 1986).

Chandra Mukerji (2010), also relying on an infrastructural example, shows however that even when political actors are initially successful in achieving their political goals by manipulating, changing, or reorganizing the material world, they may in the end find that they cannot stay fully in control. Her historical case study shows how the Canal du Midi that was constructed in the seventeenth century in the south of France, connecting the Mediterranean Sea with the Atlantic Ocean, decreased the power of local nobility vis-à-vis the king, Louis XIV. The nobility could not benefit from the canal (since it had been banned from engaging in trade) and also saw the erosion of its power over local craftsmen, farmers, traders, and village women, who now found new sources of economic livelihood facilitated by water transport and the reliable availability of water for various economic activities such as laundering, irrigation, and weaving. At the same time, due to their lack of scientific understanding, local nobility could not interfere with the location, size, or other physical aspects of the canal; those appeared to have been simply determined by technical rationality and thus came to embody an impersonal power. Mukerji calls this *logistical* power. The nobility found that its traditional political tools (such as making and breaking alliances, using ideology, cajoling, intimidation, or coercion, modes of domination Mukerji calls *strategic* power) could not match logistical power. The Sun King not only increased his tax revenues from the novel economic activities along the Canal du Midi, but also extended his power over territories that previously he could only control with the help of local nobility. Eventually, however, Louis XIV realized that this new type of power resided not in his person—as is the case with traditional strategic power—but in his administration, and thus his individual influence was lessened. Ultimately, he solved this problem by disgracing the key architects of the project, by resorting to the traditional political tools of strategic power. The point is not that logistical power always wins out over strategic power—after all, those holding only logistical power, the architects and the other experts working for them, lost out in the end—but that, historically, logistical power became more important, so that those who could engage in both held an upper hand.

Mukerji argues that infrastructure—not only canals, but also roads, and later dams, railroads, electricity grids, and phone lines—facilitated the centralization of power that was less and less strategic and more and more logistical, ultimately laying down the sociomaterial foundations of the modern territorial nation-state.

Actor-network theory has retained the importance of nonhuman actors, but questions society's ability to fully determine the outcome of sociomaterial assemblages. In its view, while powerful entities can indeed create networks of human and nonhuman actors, this network can move in unintended and unanticipated ways, so that maintaining it is hard work, which renders any power inherently fragile (Latour 2005). Latour's case of speed bumps (1994), which in many European languages are called "sleeping" or "reclining policemen," is one of four ways in which technology mediates human or social action. Latour argues that by implementing speed bumps, whichever authority—the police, the chancellor of his university, or the municipal government—delegates capacity to an object, so that the action of compelling drivers to slow down is redistributed away from humans to nonhumans. Besides being more efficient—no need to pay a policeman to stand guard day and night—this delegation however has another important advantage. As Latour says,

> The relative ordering of presence and absence is redistributed—we hourly encounter hundreds, even thousands, of absent makers who are remote in time and space yet simultaneously active and present. And through such detours, finally, the political order is subverted, since I rely on many delegated actions that themselves make me do things *on behalf of others who are no longer here and that I have not elected* and the course of whose existence I cannot even retrace. (Latour 1994, 40, my emphasis)

This is probably the most political of Latour's statements. In it he comes close to admitting that, contrary to his insistence on power as fragile and always emergent, nonhuman actors, objects, standardized practices, or a particular organization of space can be employed strategically by humans, or their collectives, to achieve political goals or to resolve social problems, albeit in a much less transparent way than if the resolution took place in the more visible realm of public discourse and democratic fora of deliberation. It is this "action at a distance" that is key for our understanding of the relationship between materiality and power.

ANT needs this idea of action at a distance to provide a horizontal alternative to social scientists' usual conceptualization of power relations as vertical. The insistence on understanding power as a matter of the length of links and connections in a network of actors is necessary because ANT's representatives, most explicitly Latour, insist on the social having a flat topography. For him society is a "flattened-out" landscape, made up of human and nonhuman actors and their linkages. While, to its credit, ANT's use of the network metaphor to capture the nature of society is much more attentive to the *making* of these linkages than those globalization scholars who also use the concept of network—an application I have critiqued (Gille and O'Riain 2002; Gille 2006)—it still retains some weaknesses associated with the flatness or the two-dimensionality of the concept. One is the assumed ephemerality of the connections among nodes; the other is the absence of the scalar differentiation of nodes as well as linkages.

For ANT, the elimination of the micro-macro distinction translates into restricting empirical research to the micro level and denying the existence of the macro scale altogether. Another posthumanist sociologist, Andrew Pickering (1995), in a different way, argues that rather than assuming an a priori macro level, our task as social scientists is to demonstrate how the macro emerges from the micro. He shows that what he calls "the mangle"—the back and forth between social intentions and their material realizations—occurs at the level of the macro as well. In the only empirical reference to the macro I have found in his work, he claims that the intersection of science and the military in World War II demonstrates how science made itself a macro actor. This interpretation of the macro emerging from the micro is insufficient to the extent that it is various macro-level events (the war for example) that opened the "macro door" to science, events that are not, however, analyzed as such. There may be newly emerged macro actors, but the roles previously emerged macro-level events, relations, and dynamics play in the birth of a new macro actor are missing.

Furthermore, there is no theoretical room, here or in other ANT studies, to discern if these macro-level dynamics are qualitatively different from those at the micro level. Law (2007) makes this explicit when concluding, from the equal ease of dialing 911 and launching tanks in Kabul, that "the same relational logics apply at any scale" (no page). But his admission of black-boxing and other strategies of making assemblages durable seems to contradict the assumed sameness of micro and macro dynamics. For example, explaining the historical inequality of "the West and the Rest," Latour and Law see the West's superiority as lying in its practice of having "accumulated a series of small and practical techniques that generate cumulative advantage" (Law 2007, no page). Black-boxing, cumulative advantages, and Law's concept of "teleologically ordered patterns of relations indifferent to human intention" (no page) all point to the relative autonomy of the macrosocial.

To understand the power of entities and actors we generally locate at the macro or global scales, ANT argues that we just need to follow the links to farther and farther nodes in the network. ANT does this with the explicit goal of avoiding the danger its proponents see in the social sciences, namely the reification of power and what they call the black-boxing of the market, capitalism, or even globalization. But reification is a matter of abstraction, not of social scale, and for this reason we must conclude that ANT too has bought wholesale into the identification of the macro level with abstraction and the micro level with concreteness.

Law (2004) seemingly eschews this problem. Not only does he problematize the concept of network—because it is still grounded in the belief in a bounded whole—but he also talks of varying degrees of complexity as one travels down or up the rungs of social scale. He does not so much deny that the macro or the global exist as argue that the micro and the local tend to be more complex than the macro/global, and that the global can be contained within the local. That said, he too urges a move to the micro with the belief that the macro is less concrete, and for him higher levels of abstraction are problematic inasmuch as they prevent us from appreciating the true—even if ever-elusive—complexity of the world. Thus he too conflates social scale with level of abstraction. This deserves a bit more attention.

As we have seen, even the market can be the product of many determinations—that is, a concrete entity. This however is not the same as arguing that it does not exist at the macro or global levels or that some actors cannot use it and even mold it to their advantage more than others can, as ANT would like us to believe (Peck 2013). Economic sociologists and institutionalist economists have long demonstrated the social construction of the market, and Timothy Mitchell (2002) shows how it is produced in both colonial and postcolonial Egypt. The conclusion to draw from these studies is not that there is no such thing as the market, but that once it is in place as a mechanism of power, it can get entrenched and can extend and "govern at a distance" relatively independently from those who set it in motion. An important aspect of power is exactly how it manages to traverse scales and reproduce itself in different concrete situations. ANT makes gestures toward such an understanding when it coins phrases such as "centers of calculation," "immutable mobiles," or "translation," but its actual analysis always remains at the micro level. It does not recognize that once macro dynamics or macro actors emerge from micro-level ones, they can become relatively autonomous from their micro foundations, and temporally enduring. As Noel Castree correctly puts it, they may develop an ability to "collect power and condense it," and thereby compel other actors to act as "intermediaries" or act on their behalf (Castree 2002, 141). Their endurance, and their ability to act as intermediaries, is made possible exactly by being embroiled in new macro configurations. Exactly in order to tease out the political implications, we have to focus on the global scale but keep our attention on the concrete and the material. An aspect of the new modality of power is to upscale certain materialities while blocking others.

Recent uses of ANT have tried to engage with politics and power in more nuanced ways. A key contribution of this literature has been to demonstrate that publics are not pre-existing, but often are "sparked into being" by a specific material entity (Barry 2001; Marres 2012; Braun and Whatmore 2010). Marres (2012), channeling John Dewey, even sees this phenomenon as potentially progressive and empowering, because, as she demonstrates with the example of carbon meters, the use of objects generates more traditional forms of political activism, such as participation in public discourse, voting, lobbying, and so forth. Her concept of material participation aims to debunk the old assumption that mundane, practical ways of responding to a social problem are ineffectual and prevent "real" political engagement.

Ulrich Beck (1992), though not usually considered a proponent of the material and practice turn, has also called attention to a new relationship between materiality and politics. In his classic book, he argues that we live in a society where risks have taken on a qualitatively new nature. In contrast to "old risks," today we cannot say we willingly and knowingly assume risks; the air I breathe may be full of contaminants, of which I am not only unaware, but which I was never asked whether I wanted to risk breathing. Part of the reason we are caught unawares is because today's risks are not visible or easily accessible to our senses. Instead we increasingly rely on experts to tell us whether the particulates in our air are below a safe threshold. Finally, the same modern hygienic technologies we think are there to protect us can themselves become new sources of health hazards, for example antibiotics, chlorine, and many other chemicals we use for cleaning in our households. Beck argues that the political reaction to these new risks has been profound. First, the heightened sense of being exposed without knowing it until it is too late gives rise to "catastrophic politics" that can be a potent obstacle to rational deliberation. Second, the political goal in the new "risk society" is less to receive a larger share of the pie (the distribution of goods) and more and more to be protected from risks (distribution of "bads"). Finally, there is a perception that our existing forms of democracy and social institutions are not capable of protecting us from these ever-newer risks, and thus people increasingly shift their activism to the subpolitical level, by engaging directly with the materiality that seems so threatening: they eat only certain foods, use certain building materials and cleaning supplies, and drive certain vehicles.

If these authors, coming from quite different theoretical backgrounds, all converge on the thesis that there is a fundamentally new relationship between materiality and politics, should we not feel justified in extending their analysis to the European Union? And what would that application look like?

One possible thesis could be that the European Union has reacted to this shift to the subpolitical by legislating an increasing number of safety and environmental standards, and indeed this has been the dominant explanation for the proliferation of standards and the so-called reflexivity turn in policy making. But this does not explain why only certain concerns are reacted to in this way: why for example anxiety over aflatoxin levels in imported spice peppers or the extreme alkalinity of red mud did not result in elevated standards. Another form of application of these theories of material politics is that technological zones and particular sociomaterial assemblages lower transaction costs and are functional for free trade in the EU. While this may explain some of the developments in policy making and standard setting, it not only elides the previous question of selectiveness, but it also obscures whose standards and whose technologies will become the normative foundations for these zones. These two interpretations assume that there is a pre-existing public with pre-existing interests, whether in lowering risks or in free trade, which brings its issues up for public deliberation. We could argue, however, with Marres (2012), that the public of the European Union, to the extent that there is such a collective, has been only brought to life by specific concerns. Indeed, this could be an alternative interpretation of the opening statement by the chairman of the European Parliament's Committee on the Environment, Public Health and Consumer Protection in a 1996 hearing on mad cow disease: "if the European Community had not existed before the BSE crisis, it would have had to be invented" (Collins 1996). While Collins' point was that this is a quintessentially cross-border problem necessitating a supranational solution, we could go further and argue that prior to the crisis, there was little evidence of an EU public. Such a perspective can be helpful in explaining the heightened importance given to food safety legislation in the conditionalities of postsocialist countries' EU membership. Theoretical consistency then also requires, however, that we see reactions in those countries to EU safety and other agricultural standards as also engendering a public, a different public from the BSE-generated one. This public has been animated not so much by food safety risks but rather by the economic risks arising from dealing with food safety in new ways.[5] What does the relationship between materiality and EU-level politics look like from their perspective?

THE MATERIALIZATION OF POLITICS

For decades, the European Union has been plagued by agricultural overproduction. Butter mountains and lakes of milk or wine are just the best-known metaphors for this situation. Yet for the postsocialist countries, a key appeal of EU membership was increasing their access to lucrative food markets, in which they could easily compete thanks to their considerably lower labor costs. The conditionalities of EU membership—production quotas, farm subsidies that were lower than previous entrants enjoyed and had their own conditionalities, the elimination of state subsidies to the food industry—went a long way toward eliminating such a competitive advantage. But what made it possible to go beyond this, and even increase not only the competitive advantage but also the market share for western European food companies in eastern Europe, was the extensive system of elaborate food safety, quality, and ethical standards. An apple grower I interviewed complained that in order to receive farm subsidies, he had to buy specific seeds and had to plant his trees at a given distance from each other. Another apple grower said he could only sell apples of specific sizes and grown with a particular Dutch pesticide that fulfilled the requirements of integrated pest management. Guntra Aistara (2011) demonstrates how Latvian organic farmers suffered from the EU requirement that they use specific seeds, not only seeds that were certified organic but that were certified to be seeds, which not only prevented them from using and exchanging their own seeds, but elevated their production costs. Elizabeth Dunn (2005) shows that if Polish farmers wanted to keep slaughtering their own pigs they would now have to implement a number of changes in their practices:

> [T]he surface and color of the wall is specified by law, as are the flooring, doors, employee locker rooms, number of wash basins, and type of wash basin taps. Walls must separate raw and finished materials, locker rooms may not open onto work rooms, and there must be a separate room for storing detergents. There are rules about the transportation infrastructure as well: how live animals may be transported is prescribed in the SPSS [Sanitary and Phytosanitary Standards], as well as the transportation of finished meat products. But along with physical infrastructure, the SPSS also mandate particular forms of documentation, tracking, and audit. Under the Integrated Administration and Control System (IACS), each animal, farm, abattoir, processing plant, and individual piece of meat must have a number, and those numbers must be recorded so that the path of each piece of meat from farm to table can be traced by inspectors or auditors. The length of time that documentation on each piece of meat must be archived for is also specified by law. (Dunn 2005, 178)

While one could understand that attention to all these details is necessary when one is building an abattoir from scratch, it is harder to accept that they are all necessary when there is a well-functioning regulatory system in place. After all, it is not that slaughtering, transportation, and general hygiene had not been regulated at all in Poland or that the rules didn't work prior to EU accession. Instead, what happened in all areas—from apples to pigs—is that EU officials deemed that prior regulation incorrect. This was yet another area in which, to quote Böröcz (2001), the European Commission turned difference into inferiority.

Dunn (2003, 2005), Aistara (2011), and Diana Mincyte (2011) have demonstrated that in the realm of agriculture all these standards have aimed not so much at increasing food safety and quality as at (a) eliminating "inefficient" small farms, (b) increasing land concentration, and (c) facilitating the consolidation of food processors and thereby making smaller farmers of "idiosyncratic" produce even more vulnerable. A Hungarian agricultural expert, who after accession also held a high-ranking position in the Ministry of Agriculture and Rural Development, argued that these outcomes are favored by the EU because they make way for large-scale industrial agriculture producing wheat and industrial crops cheaply for western European markets, while the production of more high-value-added produce—such as fruits and certain vegetables, as well as organic food—will take place mostly in the West (personal interview, 2007). My two agricultural case studies, on paprika and foie gras, can thus also be seen as cases of products that do not fit into this plan and of how such products fare in this regulatory environment.

The red mud case is both similar and different. On the one hand, regulatory harmonization here did not favor Western competitors directly, but it did express a lack of interest in protecting Hungarian society. The watering down of the criteria for the hazardous waste list in Hungary, despite decades of regulating red mud as hazardous, and the derogation period in adopting the EU's waste governance policies created a vacuum in oversight, so that the warning signs of the impending spill went unnoticed. After the disaster, instead of returning to a stricter waste policy, the whole production process had to be overhauled, a change that brought with it the mentioned unintended consequences of, first, more pollution due to the dry technology; second, cleanup contracts to Western firms; and third, the bankruptcy of MAL. One wonders whether staying with the wet technology but with greater surveillance by the various environmental authorities would have been cheaper and more protective of local residents' already strained health.

Categorizing red mud as hazardous waste at the EU level clearly went against the interests of western European aluminum producers. For them, who generate a less alkaline byproduct, categorizing red mud as hazardous waste would have been "overkill" and would have resulted in superfluous environmental expenditures. To be sure, any added expenditure could spell doom for an industry that, according to one of its main mouthpieces, the European Aluminum Association (EAA), is suffering from unfair competition from those countries that have not implemented climate-change-mitigating regulation. According to the EAA, the European Emission Trading System imposes a tax-like burden on the industry due to the high percentage of electricity costs, primarily incurred during smelting, among all production expenditures. In contrast, in countries where environmental standards are lower, competitors can continue to produce more cheaply and increase their share—which actually has already been increasing—of the European aluminum market. The EAA has been lobbying various EU fora for compensation, arguing that since its sale price is set by the London Metals Exchange, it cannot pass on the costs of environmental remediation to its consumers. At a time when other environmental regulations, such as REACH, are being newly implemented or even extended, in the case of Seveso Directive—aimed at the prevention of industrial disasters as explained in chapter 3—it would indeed be difficult to tighten yet another policy, in this case hazardous waste legislation. That representatives of the aluminum industry consider red mud regulation off the table is evident from the EAA's 2012 sustainability report (European Aluminum Association 2013), which doesn't mention red mud or any industry byproducts at all, and the only context in which the word "waste" occurs is in relation to the recycling rates of aluminum cans.

The early western European members of the EU laid the foundation of community-wide regulation that represented the technological and environmental needs of their producers. When former socialist countries entered, rather than retaining policies that reflected their economic and physical needs, they adopted EU-level policies, albeit sometimes with a temporal lag; when it was found that those were inappropriate and ineffective, as also proved to be the case in the paprika story, it was production that had to be changed to match practices of the EU-15—of the European Union as it existed before the Eastern Enlargement—of course at the producers' own expense. Not only were these expenses not "calculated in" to the balance sheet of gains and losses of EU membership, more importantly, the EU-15's sociomaterial assemblage, embodied in its particular alumina technology, was in effect "subsidized" to the extent that stricter regulations now made advisable by the entry of Hungary were averted, while Hungarian producers had no choice but to adopt the EU-15's regulations. In the foie gras case, however, the resistance of a powerful member, France, to any potential regulation or ban on force-feeding animals ensured that Hungary would be spared the consequences of having to adjust to the regulatory standards of the majority of the member states, namely those banning foie gras production.[6] To put this another way, decisions about whose sociomaterial assemblage is reflected in community-level policy, and thus who has to "reassemble" its network of humans and nonhumans to match said policies, are also decisions about whose livelihoods are prioritized.[7]

We have arrived at the point where it is necessary to name this type of politics. It used to be that legislators, following some public deliberation, designed policy that, ideally, responded to some human and social need. The policy would then necessitate that economic actors implement changes in their technologies and raw materials. That is, in most cases, we started with the realm of politics and ended in the realm of the material. Today the order is reversed. Legislators, but even more so unelected committees (Chalmers and Chaves 2014), prescribe not policy goals—"big" objectives—but actual technologies and materials to be used, and indeed they may even prescribe the physical qualities of the final product, such as the exact curvature, length, or knobbiness of produce. Those who already operate with those physical parameters will clearly get a boost from such policies. This is clearly not the result of market competition; it is a well-known effect of the phenomenon political scientists and legal scholars call regulatory capture. Similar assistance to an enterprise, industry, or a country previously would have required deliberation on economic policy reflecting regional, sectoral, and social priorities and mostly would have fallen within the competence of national governments. In today's EU, those policies are set at the community—meaning supranational—level, and one of the few ways such priorities can be realized is by prescribing the materiality of the related economic activities, rather than through normal political procedures. If, let's say, the political goal is to reduce the number and ratio of farmers in the population of a new EU member country, that objective is no longer explicitly deliberated upon in either national or European parliaments. Such a goal would obviously generate resistance and would make for lengthy deliberation. Instead, such material conditions that farmers cannot afford are simply required, and thus they will be compelled to leave agriculture. In sum, political goals have been achieved not with political tools but rather by material means. Politics has in effect been materialized.

What are the implications of the materialization of politics for democracy and social justice? Could we not say that whatever the policy and political processes involved, at least the final product—safer, higher quality food, the humane treatment of animals, or the long overdue modernization of the production technology of the aluminum industry—is worth it? Should we not applaud at least the increased regulatory oversight in matters of health and the environment? Could we not see this massive set of practical and material responses as evidence of Karl Polanyi's (1944) double movement, the almost spontaneous self-protection of society in the face of unbridled market forces that threaten not only what he called the social fabric, but also its health and long-term survival? Could materialization be an efficient way of re-embedding the economy in society, of subordinating economic rationality to social values and human needs?

Appealing as such an interpretation might be, if he were living today, Polanyi might be the first to answer in the negative. While politics may be increasingly materialized with the slogan of protecting, if not society, at least consumers, he would note that the tools of such a defense have themselves become the problem. There is a striking similarity between the process by which land, money, and people came to be treated as if they were commodities in nineteenth-century Europe and the contemporary rendering of regulation as a fictitious commodity. Just as there are negative social, economic, and environmental consequences arising from treating land, money, and people as if they were produced for the market and subjecting them to the dynamic of supply and demand—rather than recognizing that they have an existence that is both independent from the market and is more primary than the market—there are negative social consequences of treating regulation as if it were a commodity. To the extent that regulation now comes in the form of standardization and auditable packages of practices made obligatory for all producers who want to stay in business and for countries that want to enter the European Union, and to the extent that such new sociomaterial assemblages can now be bought and sold on the market, regulation itself has turned into a fictitious commodity. And while, for example, the price, quantity, and quality of HACCP workshops, certification, and audits can all be subject to the balance of supply and demand, regulation, as a public good itself, should not be treated as a commodity.

In order to understand this better, we may need to go beyond Polanyi's perspective. Nancy Fraser (2013), the feminist political philosopher, has critiqued the very foundation of Polanyi's disembedding framework. She argues that Polanyi had a naïve view of society when he assumed that all re-embedding is socially beneficial. Historical examples demonstrate that disembedding—liberating the market from social norms and values—can empower social groups whose livelihood had previously been subject to exclusions on religious, ethnic, or cultural grounds. While society, for example, may shun women's paid employment outside the home, once the economy is no longer subject to such gender norms—because it becomes disembedded from society—there is an improvement in social justice for women. By the same token, not all re-embedding guarantees fairness, empowerment, or social justice. What type of society we re-embed the economy in—whose protection from the market we prioritize—matters greatly for social justice.

When regulation shifts from political deliberation to practical and physical prescription, it becomes much less transparent whose sociomaterial assemblage has been declared the new norm, and therefore whose protection from the market has been prioritized. Normally, such questions of fairness and social priorities would be contested in public fora: parliaments, parliamentary committees, the Directorates of the EU, public hearings, media debates, etc. Today, however, such political conflicts are evaded, because the material, practical norms, and standards are presented as scientifically derived and as such apolitical.

This thesis is seemingly just a newer illustration of Latour's speed bumps (1994), the mentioned Marcusian concept of power as (technologically rational) management, or, more recently, of Chandra Mukerji's (2010) concept of logistical power. While conceptualizing the materialization of politics as these already-identified techniques of power is not incorrect, what makes a new interpretation necessary is the new types of actors by whom, and the new scales at which, these techniques are employed.

Furthermore, this action at a distance enjoys more durability than Latour and other ANT scholars would like to admit.

The Frankfurt School, while in general operating with an impersonal concept of power derived from technical rationality that was seemingly undiscerning in the subjects of domination, did tend to focus on capital's ability to harness such techniques in its own interest.[8] Mukerji's (2010) historical work on the birth of logistical power, in contrast, focuses on the state. The three case studies in this book demonstrate the emergence of not just new actors who deploy material politics, such as nongovernmental and supranational organizations, but a new relationship among "old" actors.

An early description and critique of this new power constellation came from Gary Gereffi, Ronie Garcia-Johnson, and Erika Sasser (2001), who provocatively called it the NGO-industrial complex. This concept, originally born of the study of voluntary codes of conduct, identified a new role for NGOs in designing and enforcing various certification schemes for corporations, whether in labor or environmental matters. Such certifications, they argued, cannot help but reflect and even strengthen the circumstances in which they were born, namely the hegemony of neoliberalism: free trade, deregulation, and the decline of state-provided protections for workers and the environment. These authors also called attention to the negative effect of codes of conduct on global inequalities. Such global inequalities were primarily presented as deriving from the action of multinational corporations and transnational NGOs and much less from supranational agencies. Though the article mentioned the UN's Global Compact, there is a fundamental difference between the UN's and the European Union's agency. The former's endorsement of a code is simply that: an endorsement, a recommendation. The EU's, however, is a condition of participation in the common market. While legal scholars call EU codes and standards quasi-legislative (Chalmers and Chaves

2014), in the sense that they do not arise from the actions of the European Parliament or the Council—the EU's two lawmaking bodies—they do carry the force of law.

Students of EU policies and legal structures have explained the rise of this type of regulation by reference to the increasingly cumbersome decision-making process of an ever-enlarging EU, or to other pressures that necessitated regulation to become more efficient (Chalmers and Chaves 2014). Even if we accept that the materialization of politics was primarily motivated by such administrative concerns, we cannot ignore that other consequences resulted, consequences that tilted the playing field in the favor of powerful Western producers. To be sure, we are well advised to be careful with explanations that may come across as conspiratorial, and yet we cannot dispense with our obligation as social scientists to describe and name this new modality of transnational power.

In 2014, a liberal commentator on a Hungarian TV show reacted to the conservative government's repeated call for waging a freedom struggle against Western colonizers and the bureaucrats of Brussels by visualizing a hypothetical scenario in which rich bankers exchange ideas with EU officials behind closed doors—fat cigars and expensive drinks in hand— about how to stick it even more to poor Hungarians. This hyperbolic image is effective in ridiculing any claim of Western oppression of the East. Postsocialist liberal politicians, and not only in Hungary, have not just refuted a particular interpretation of East-West inequalities—beyond absolute wealth, of economic opportunity—but refuted their existence altogether. For these politicians, to the extent that such inequalities did exist, they were simply residual and temporary and would soon be eliminated, not despite the European Union but exactly because of and with the help of it. They see increasing rural poverty, rising unemployment, and even the growing economic gap between western Europe and Hungary since accession as the result of corruption and the incompetence of those in charge of managing enterprises or the economy as a whole. In friendly debates with Hungarian liberals or leftists, I often hear the argument that it is not the EU to be blamed but the "inane" CEOs, farmers, and politicians who could not reap all the benefits of EU membership that were there for the taking. "Just look at all the financial support we receive from the European Union; we could not build new roads or rebuild our sewage system if it weren't for EU," they say. The suggestion is clearly that it is Hungarians' fault that they couldn't make good use of this support.

The New Right could emerge in Hungary following EU accession because an increasing number of Hungarians had had enough, not only of liberals' unwillingness to address inequalities between western Europe and Hungary, but also of the argument that they themselves have done everything wrong and that despite Western tutelage they have failed. Instead of denying economic grievances and new inequalities within the EU, social scientists must provide alternative interpretations of their origins, not in order to strengthen the right wing but to combat it.

Instead of seeing Hungarians as victims of the West, as the right wing does—especially evident in FIDESZ's slogan that "we will not be a colony" —scholars, activists, and politicians must start developing mechanisms by which consequential decisions about the regulation of production and consumption are made transparent and the people making those decisions are made accountable. This politicization of the material is one key tool by which we can diminish right wing voters' conviction that the EU is a rigged game and channel their justified grievances toward socially just, progressive, and more practical solutions.

NOTES

INTRODUCTION

1. According to a 1991 survey, the majority of successful private businesses had started up already in the 1980s (Lengyel 2012, 46). Building on this head start, Hungary demonstrated a spectacularly rapid increase in entrepreneurial activity in the first few years of the transition. The number of newly registered Ltds. jumped from 455 in 1988 to 18,000 in 1990 (Lengyel 2012, 69), and in 1993, 870,000 people worked in the sphere of small enterprise (Czakó et al. 1995); in 1997 that figure approached one million.

2. This is measured as the ratio of the materially deprived population, which is at 26.8 percent, to the EU average of 9.6 percent. http://ec.europa.eu/eurostat/statistics -explained/index.php/Material_deprivation_statistics_-_early_results; http://www .wsws.org/en/articles/2014/01/11/hung-j11.html.

3. In 2010 it received 16.67 percent of the votes; in 2014 it received 20.54 percent.

4. The OCCRP's "person of the year" award is given annually to the individual who does the most to enable and promote organized criminal activity. http://occrp.org /person-of-the-year/2014/#runners.

5. In my earlier writings, I signaled the importance of metals for building communism with all its related and often unintended consequences with the term "metallic socialism" (Gille 2007).

6. This fact has rendered Hungarian waste statistics uniquely unsuitable for cross-national comparisons. About the problems of such comparisons in general, see Gille (2007) and chapter 3 of this book on red mud in particular.

7. See for example Cris Shore (2000).

8. To my knowledge Cris Shore (2000) was the first social scientist to undertake a scholarly analysis of these images.

9. The front side of the coins are uniform, the back sides are unique to the member state that minted them.

10. Certainly, these were the majority of the billboard ads. I only have records of three other of these types of question-and-answer posters. They posed the following questions: "Can I receive my pension in other EU countries?" "Will we be able to prevent speculative land purchases?" and, amazingly, "Are babes hot in the EU?"

11. Without providing an exhaustive list, the key authors here are Valerie Bunce (1999, 1995), Burawoy and Lukács (1992), Kristen Ghodsee (2011), Katherine Verdery (2004, 1999, 1994), David Stark (1992a, 1992b, 1990), Caroline Humphrey (1991, 1999), Michael Kennedy (2002), Krisztina Fehérváry (2013), Daphne Berdahl (1999), Steven Sampson (2002), Gerald Creed (2010, 1999), József Böröcz (1993, 1992), Judit Bodnár (2001), Elizabeth Dunn (2004), Olga Shevchenko (2009), and Katrina Schwartz (2006).

12. The "original" Great Transformation refers to the forceful introduction of a new free market capitalism in the nineteenth century that Karl Polanyi analyzed in his 1944 book with the same title.

1. THE 2004 HUNGARIAN PAPRIKA BAN

1. Though I could still find a salesperson at a small tourist stall willing to sell me a little package of paprika fancily packaged in a decorative canvas pouch. She assured me that if it was a present for foreigners it would be all right, since she assumed it would only be used for show rather than for cooking—at that price, indeed, it would have been like cooking with silver . . .

2. In the various lawsuits and legal proceedings some of the companies contested these laboratory findings.

3. Many cooperative members have private lands in cultivation as well. This is reminiscent of the arrangement from the socialist decades, when cooperative members or state farm employees still grew fruits and vegetables or kept domestic animals on their small private garden plots. The party-state initially saw such an allowance for private ownership as a way to pacify the peasantry, otherwise resentful of collective ownership; by the 1970s, however, it was clear that without the efficient little farms cultivated in a second or third shift—though in a symbiotic relationship with the state farms and cooperatives—there would be serious shortages of food. Food shortages plagued most former communist countries, but Hungary managed to evade them, especially after the economic reforms implemented in the late 1960s. This lent a legitimacy to the state socialist regime in Hungary that was greater than that of most of the Soviet bloc.

4. State socialism is the sociological term we use to describe the type of society that had dominated that part of the world since 1947–48.

5. In many cases, however, the owners of land prior to collectivization could not be found (for example, they had died or emigrated) or preferred cash to the land. The process of land reprivatization was a complicated legal project and was much contested; the details are beyond the scope of this book.

6. Though even the pre-accession period didn't see free trade in these goods.

7. Agricultural experts agreed that in setting the quotas it would have been in Hungary's interest to use the late 1990s or early 2000s consumption levels as the reference period. (1994 is considered to be the turning point.) Using the baseline of the early 1990s, when, due to the economic crisis resulting from the collapse of the state sector and unemployment, Hungarian domestic consumption of most of these goods was still low (often lower than before the collapse of state socialism), meant that future growth in demand would entail having to increase agricultural import in goods that Hungary previously had been self-sufficient in (Kiss 2001; European Commission Agricultural DG 2002, 1998; Budapest Analyses 2004).

8. Initially the reduction of advantage resulted in the EU-15 (the western European countries) having an agricultural trade surplus with Hungary through 2006. After that year the trade balance between Hungary and the EU-27 became positive, mostly due to trading with new eastern European member states, which today receive 40 percent of Hungary's agricultural exports. This prompted one study to ask whether the socialist camp's trading bloc, COMECON, is reviving itself, even if only informally.

9. This regulation was finally eliminated in 2009, but many similar ones on apples, citrus fruit, kiwi fruit, lettuces, peaches and nectarines, pears, strawberries, sweet peppers, table grapes, and tomatoes are still in place.

10. These are referred to as B2C, business-to-consumer certification schemes, and B2B, business-to-business certification schemes, respectively.

11. Most of the schemes apply to more than one area.

12. Such subsidies are part of the Common Agricultural Policy of the European Union and its legal predecessors, and their main goal has been to protect farmers from low market prices, whether domestically or internationally. They have also been used as an incentive to limit output, as mentioned, and more recently to encourage and reward farmers who implement environmentally more sustainable practices.

13. One fascinating exception to avoiding the national frame in designing the EU standard is the definition of chocolate (Cidell and Alberts 2006).

14. Before the buyout of Szeged Paprika in 2006 (about which there is more later in this chapter), the museum's web page contained such historical records. Today's version is much shorter and no longer contains them.

15. Socialist Hungary had among the most, if not the most, open economies in the socialist bloc. Earning hard currency, among other goods, by selling agricultural commodities to the West became especially important in the post-1968 reform period, for purchasing Western technologies and consumer products, and for paying back Western loans.

16. A Hungaricum is a product unique to Hungary; it is not a legal category that provides brand-name-like or geographical-indicator-type protection.

17. The United States's maximum concentration is quite a bit higher: twenty micrograms mycotoxin per kilogram of produce (Venâncio and Paterson 2007). Brazil nuts are a species of nuts, not nuts from Brazil.

18. Though a 2013 study by Hungarian scientists argues that aflatoxin is now occurring with increasing frequency in European-grown produce, especially in maize and dairy products, due to global climate change (Kocsubé et al. 2013).

19. The two key challenges of infusing traditional food preparation with modern safety practices are ensuring that these practices do not decrease "the characteristic sensory qualities of these traditional . . . products" and that they thereby do not decrease diversity (European Commission, Directorate-General for Research and Innovation 2007, 12).

20. Council Regulation (EC) No 510/2006 'Kalocsai Fűszerpaprika-Őrlemény' EC No: HU-PDO-0005-0393-21.10.2004.

21. For a Foucauldian analysis of the auditing and quality management, see Elizabeth Dunn (2004, 2005), and of HACCP specifically, Lawrence Busch (2004) and Dunn (2007).

22. Note that imported peppers enter the country in the form of dried peppers and not as already ground spice, so the portion of Brazilian paprika in the overall volume of ground Hungarian paprika was less than 1 percent at the most, if one assumes—falsely—its equal distribution in the annual production.

23. See Parliamentary Session minutes quoted in *Index* (2004) and interview with former head of Paprika Produce Council in *HVG* (2004, 95).

24. The more sunshine peppers receive before harvest, the more pigment they contain.

25. Produce Councils are corporate NGOs that not only represent the interests of their members (both producers and processors) and the segment of the food industry they work in, but also execute governmental functions, such as data collection, the administration of EU grants, the monitoring of EU production quotas, and the training of members in new safety and hygiene standards, among others.

26. Mixing is common practice in other food commodities in the EU. In 2011 the revelation that Bertolli's "Italian" olive oil contained a good proportion of African-grown olives caused consumer outrage (Mueller 2011).

27. Small producers provide 90 percent of the raw material needs for Hungary's paprika production.

28. In the conclusion I will come back to the question of why those allegedly in charge, whether in the case of paprika imports or of the red mud spill, seemed to have been caught unawares of the new regulations and their scope of authority.

29. The shorthand term used for action taken at the customs border is "border control" or "on the market."

30. Spain itself reported mycotoxins in imported peppers in only one case, in Brazilian peppers, in 2005.

31. Note that the incident occurred well before Szeged and Kalocsa paprika received PDO designations, in 2010 and 2012, respectively. Under the rules pertaining to the protected use of geographical origins in labeling and marketing, of course, the exact origins not only have to be marked, but the use of any other ingredient is also prohibited and sanctionable.

32. It is not clear from this source whether the interests of processors are seen to dominate more strongly than those of producers or than those of consumers. In my opinion, either (or both) would be a fair interpretation of the prime minister's words. The rationale for this switch in authority was that during the investigations it became clear that the national Hungarian Food Safety Bureau (MÉBH) had enough information to act much earlier: regional agencies of the main public health authority, ÁNTSZ, confiscated shipments, levied a fine on one of the processors, and launched a criminal investigation already in August, two months before the ban. It is also true, however, that MÉBH was established experimentally a couple of years before not as an authority, but rather as an agency to coordinate among various authorities, to analyze risks, and to operate the Rapid Alert System for Feed and Food (RASFF), which, according to most media analysts, it failed to do with sufficient speed (*HVG* 2004). In my interview with him just a few months prior to the paprika scandal, the director of MÉBH emphasized the same lack of authority to act.

2. THE 2008 FOIE GRAS BOYCOTT

1. The worldwide campaign's details can be found at http://www.vier-pfoten.eu /our-focus/farm-animals-2/foie-gras-2/, while the associated Hungarian organization and its Hungary-focused foie gras–related efforts can be followed at http://www.negy -mancs.hu/kampanyok/haszonallatok/kenyszertoemes-/, though a recent visit to the site (on February 13, 2015) found only information about another campaign of theirs against live feather plucking.

2. This was at the time of the boycott, in contrast to the early 2000s, when feed was the most significant expenditure (Tóásó 2006).

3. In my experience it is not so much the name Hungerit, which after all is a relatively new name for this meat processor, but its location, Szentes, that is associated in Hungarian consumers' minds with good quality products. The Szentes Meat Plant is the name most would find familiar.

4. These suits are still ongoing. Some of the lawsuits were launched by farmers, one by Hungerit, and one by the Hungarian Authority of Competition (Versenyjogi Hivatal), which claims to have evidence of suspicious business sources of the financing of FP's campaign, in the amount of about forty-five million forints (US$205,000).

5. This is corroborated by two previous nonrepresentative surveys, one conducted by a popular TV talk show (*Szempont* [Point of View]), the other an ongoing online survey maintained by Hungerit. In the former, the vast majority of people following the show and chatting online argued that people's livelihood is more important than whether geese feel pain when force-fed; in the latter the vast majority of a very small and unrepresentative sample of people considered Four Paws' actions as motivated by anti-Hungarian intent. The actual and biased wording of the web survey reported thirty-four votes for the response "Yes, I am outraged by the damage, the ignorance, the irresponsibility, and the destruction of Hungarian traditions." The argument "I agree with protecting animals but this is not that" received eight votes. Only two votes said this strategy was not anti-Hungarian. http://webszavazo.com/includes/poll/vote.php ?poll_num=4315, accessed April 14, 2009.

6. http://www.npr.org/templates/story/story.php?storyId=11032178, last accessed April 9, 2009.

7. Today, Four Paws is trying a less negative campaign by promoting a "positive list" of producers of foie gras who don't keep birds in a cage and do not apply gavage. Clicking on the link for the list, however, brings up an error page. http://www.negy-mancs.hu /kampanyok/haszonallatok/kenyszertoemes-/viziszarnyas-termel-es-feldolgozo-cegek -pozitiv-listaja/.

8. The Hungarian animal protection law explicitly excludes gavage from the category of force-feeding and thus of animal torture in general (1998. évi XXVIII. törvény, 6.§).

9. In its 2006 report, FP mentions the following countries as targeted in their anti-force-feeding campaign: Hungary, Germany, Austria, Switzerland, and the Netherlands. http://www.vierpfoten.eu/website/output.php?id=1245&language=1.

10. The group's representative also did not keep his promise to me for an interview.

11. http://www.feherkeresztliga.hu/index.php?option=com_content&view
=article&id=120%3Aa-liba-uegy-legujabb-fejlemenyei&catid=89%3Ajogi-munka&
Itemid=48&lang=en. According to Caro (2009), the modus operandi for anti–foie
gras activists in North America has been to visit and make video footage of breeding
and processing facilities undercover, which could explain FP's reticence to disclose
locations.

12. See for example http://video.google.com/videosearch?hl=en&client=firefox-a
&rls=org.mozilla:en-US:official&q=foie%20gras%20hungary&um=1&ie=UTF-8&sa
=N&tab=wv#.

13. Available at http://video.google.com/videosearch?hl=en&client=firefox-a&rls
=org.mozilla:en-US:official&q=foie%20gras%20hungary&um=1&ie=UTF-8&sa=N
&tab=wv#.

14. http://www.mtv.hu/videotar/?id=29494, last accessed April 4, 2009.

15. http://magyarliba.atw.hu/01/dark_shine/home.html, emphasis mine.

16. This view of peasants and farmers as the truest representatives of Hungarianness
is a recurring theme both in the Hungarian literary tradition—gaining special salience
between the reform era (1820s) and the 1848–49 liberation struggles against the Haps-
burg empire—and in the explicit political discourse of the interwar period, as advocated
by populist intellectuals (Esbenshade 2006). Ironically, the EU's recognition of certain
food commodities as repositories of local, regional, and occasionally national culture
in its "protected designations of origin" (PDO), "protected geographical indications"
(PGI), and "Traditional Specialty Guaranteed" (TSG) labels unintentionally reasserts
the location of Hungarianness in the agrarium (Gille 2010).

17. PETA is an exception in this regard. In 2009 this most well-known U.S. animal
rights organization issued the "foie gras challenge" that would award $10,000 to anyone
"that can produce a purely vegetarian faux foie gras comparable in taste and texture to
the real thing" (Sun 2009).

18. This is consistent with the observations of Deborah Heath and Anne Meneley
(2010).

3. THE 2010 RED MUD SPILL

1. Despite searching for months, I was not able to determine which of these countries still discharge red mud in this manner.

2. The economic advantages for Hungary in this agreement were disputed by an
analysis of the CIA (CIA Office of Current Intelligence 1952, 5) and more recently
by László Borhi (2000), hinting at a type of economic exploitation characteristic
of colonialism.

3. Some people who had experience working at MAL also attributed the weakening
of the walls to the change in the composition of the gray ash, another byproduct of the
plant, which had been used as the main ingredient of the walls.

4. Of all wastes generated in production, distribution, and consumption, including
agricultural waste (which is for the most part recovered in agriculture and is mainly
of plant origin), less than 5 percent is hazardous waste, amounting to 3.4 million tons
annually (National Waste Management Plan 2003–2008).

5. Although at that point the dry-stacking process was just being implemented in western Europe, in Hungary a more rudimentary version, in which the red mud was partly dried without the sophisticated procedures implemented later in the West, had been practiced since 1972.

6. Szirmai and Lehocki demonstrate that this was because the alumina factory failed to cover ponds nos. 6 and 7 with plants, as instructed by environmental authorities.

7. Eventually these ponds were recultivated, which reduced the dust pollution.

8. The reservoirs nearest to the Danube are ponds nos. 4–7 at Almásfüzitő, adjacent to the country's northern border with Slovakia.

9. MAL, in a criticism of this report, objected to the fact that the committee had not asked for testimony by geotechnics experts, who presumably would have confirmed MAL's explanation of the disaster.

10. Seveso III was to come into force in 2015; see below.

11. MAL was correct in arguing that Hungarian Academy of Sciences experts have signed on to the nonhazardousness of red mud, but, according to the investigations of the Parliamentary Committee, the samples on which the ruling was issued came from ponds nos. 1–9, many of which had dried to much lower levels of alkalinity or had stored drier residue to begin with (Jávor and Hargitai 2011).

12. This fact, by the way, allowed right-wing interpreters to make the connection between communism and the red mud spill, in which they were further aided by a peculiarity of the Hungarian language, which has two words for the color red. One is *piros* and the other, the one used for the red mud, is *vörös*, referring to a deep or flaming red. People with red hair, for example, are said to have *vörös haj* (hair); the flames of fire are also *vörös* and so is the symbolic color of socialists and communists. As an example see this little "poem" that was circulated in Hungarian cyberspace in the wake of the disaster: "*Trianon/Vörös terror/Árvízek/Viharláncok/Vörös iszap*" ("Trianon/Red Terror/Floods/Chains of Storms/Red Mud"). http://mr-moto-velorex.blogspot.com/2010/10/utanam-voros-iszap.html.

13. MAL, in its response to the report of the Parliamentary Committee investigating the disaster, argued that this is a misleading figure to the extent that the new owner actually also paid some debts of HUNGALU (the name of the company prior to privatization), which amounted to about 433 million forints. This still means that the new owners paid less than one four-hundredth of the nominal value of the company's capital stock. MAL, however, points out that the international accounting firm KPMG valued the company as worth negative (!) 700 million forints.

14. MAL disputes this (ATV 2011).

15. This salination danger is due to the high sodium content of red mud, which in turn comes from the NaOH liquid used in alumina production, as described above.

16. A study conducted on the spilled sludge confirmed the presence of REEs (Mayes et al. 2011).

17. I actually interviewed Bakonyi already in 1996 to gather information about the history of Hungary's waste policies.

18. Although it adds, "at the same time it reduces the environmental potential," by which it probably meant that the activity would not result in the environmentally more desirable recultivation of the territories in question.

19. Initially, Hennon suggested that if Hungary wants to press for tighter controls in the wake of the Ajka ecological disaster, the EU is prepared to listen. "We are open to looking at all European legislation, whether it can be tightened." http://affleap.com/hungarys-ecological-disaster-a-flaw-in-eu-regulations/. I found no record anywhere, however, that such discussions or such an investigation took place.

20. Seveso III, which was to come into force in 2015, was primarily made necessary by a new classificatory system of chemicals (CLP, Classification, Labelling and Packaging), which in turn was necessary to comply with the UN's Globally Harmonised System (GHS). There is no major change from Seveso II, though the scope of EU inspections is expanded and the public is supposed to receive more information and opportunity for participation.

21. Note that state socialism itself was defined as embodying different types of incongruities, which in turn produced particular ailments (Casals 1980; Hankiss 1984, 1990; Kornai 1990; Mandel 1974; Ticktin 1992a, 1992b).

22. Formalist theories of existing socialism presume that unless societies are held together by an overarching, integrating logic (whether it's called principle of organization, rationality, systemic paradoxes, or goal function), they cannot reproduce themselves, at least not in the long run. Thus they explained the many problems and crisis tendencies of former socialist countries—such as shortages, lack of innovation, or hoarding—with coexisting but logically mutually exclusive mechanisms, usually that of the market and central planning (Ticktin 1992a, 1992b; Staniszkis 1992; Fehér, Heller, and Márkus 1983; Hankiss 1990; Kornai 1990).

4. NEOLIBERALISM, MOLECULARIZATION, AND THE SHIFT TO GOVERNANCE

1. Moss argues that his work is not concerned with whether development works, but *how* it works.

2. Nevertheless, there is a numerical truth to this zero-sum claim. The number of laws regulating the market far outweighs those aimed at "bigger" and loftier issues, such as freedom and justice (Chalmers and Chaves 2014, 158–59).

3. By bigness she means both its generality and scale, corresponding to how I use the terms "levels of abstraction" and "social scale" in the introductory chapter.

4. This rhymes with what Richard Wilk (1995) called the shift from local to global structures of difference. In a seminal article, Wilk argued that globalization consists less of the homogenization of culture than that of the criteria or categories across which cultural difference is distributed.

5. See Jamie Peck's thoughtful review of different ways of "explaining with neoliberalism" (Peck 2013).

6. During this period there has also been intense research and elaboration of new comprehensive animal welfare legislation. In 2006, for the first time, the Community Action Plan on the Protection and Welfare of Animals 2006–2010, adopted by the European Commission, grouped and systematized the various aspects of EU policy on animal welfare governing the keeping of billions of animals for economic purposes in the EU. EC 2012. http://ec.europa.eu/food/animal/welfare/actionplan/docs/aw_strategy_19012012_en.pdf.

7. The European Union launched the EU Emissions Trading System (EU ETS) in 2005 as the cornerstone of its strategy for cutting emissions of carbon dioxide (CO_2) and other greenhouse gases. As one of the most energy-intensive industries, aluminum production falls under this scheme. The regulation that concerns aluminum cans is the EU Directive on Packaging Waste, legislated in 1994.

8. Which is not to say that standardization itself had been missing from their agenda beforehand. In fact, one could say that even classical sociology—Marx and Weber, in particular—and neo-Durkheimians have touched on standardization as integrally linked with modernization and capitalism (for an overview see Timmermans and Epstein [2010]).

9. Other, non-UN-affiliated studies of this trend include Pimbert et al. (2001); Government Office for Science (2011); and Agriculture and Natural Resources Team of the UK Department for International Development (2004).

10. While the latter seems to provide more transparency than the other three, in practice MSIs can often be hijacked by the strongest "members" in the initiative.

11. More recently this claim has been contested (Kimura 2013).

12. Flexible accumulation is used to describe the most recent phase of capitalism that is characterized by, among other factors, the small-batch production of a large variety of product types produced for an ever more fragmented market, companies with little or no inventories, flexible employment relations and the ensuing decline of labor unions, the increasing proportion of profit resulting from financial services (rather than from manufacturing or the main profile of a company), and more horizontal firm organization. For a full discussion see Harvey (1990).

13. A related shift has been a requirement for development and conservation projects of the World Bank and other organizations to include civil actors. This participatory model has come under much scrutiny (Cooke and Kothari 2001; Kapoor 2005).

14. See Todorova (1997); Wolff (1994).

15. Such projects have been described by more studies than I can refer to here (Kennedy and Gianoplus 1994; Wedel 1998; Marody and Giza-Poleszczuk 2000; Bessenyey-Williams 2001; Lipschutz 1996; Dunn 2004, 2005).

16. While other terms could replace the term "figured world" when the emphasis is on the cultural and imaginative construction of reality—such as "framing" or "cultural models"—Holland et al. emphasize the relative durability and material nature of the type of constellations through which people make sense of events and phenomena, and which in turn materially shape them. "Figured world" thus captures more precisely the way Hungarians and Romanians, for example, recognize themselves and the West. A good example of figured world is Mukerji's (2010) of U.S. freeways, though she tweaks the concept to talk of figured worlds of power.

CONCLUSION

1. For a good start on such an overview, see Geismar (2011) and Coole and Frost (2010); for a more involved and more philosophically oriented one see Bennett (2010).

2. For overviews of how philosophical stances relate to acknowledging the agency of materiality, see Latour (1993a, 1993b); Pickering (2001); Coole and Frost (2010); MacKenzie (1984); Bennett (2010); and Foster (1999).

3. A similar product is corn, whose material qualities made it not only an excellent source of many key substances for the settlers of North America, but also rendered it a universal equivalent—that is, money (Pollan 2006).

4. Since neo-Marxist analysis, by default, doesn't conceive of materiality at the transnational or global scale, I will not include it here, but key scholars that prefer a Marxist revalorization of nonhuman actors in the social sciences are Foster (2000); Castree (2002); Rudy (2005); Gareau (2005); and Fine (2005).

5. I have written elsewhere about the prevalent use of the concept of risk, in which economic uncertainty is excluded (Gille 2013).

6. Though Hungary was not spared the economic consequences of the boycott by FP.

7. Here I am paraphrasing Susanne Freidberg's beautiful argument that "the question of where food should come from [supplied locally or globally] is also a question about whose food provisioning and livelihoods we should care about" (2004, 31).

8. Though later, in Habermas' (1970) work, the state itself becomes the key agent of power.

REFERENCES

168 óra (168 Hours). 2011. "Illés: a MAL Zrt. már nem akarta tovább fenntartani a tevékenységét" (Illés: MAL did not want to continue its activity). http://www.168ora.hu /itthon/illes-a-mal-zrt-mar-nem-akarta-tovabb-fenntartani-a-tevekenyseget-71514 .html.

Agriculture and Natural Resources Team of the UK Department for International Development. 2004. *Concentration in Food Supply and Retail Chains.* http://dfid-agri culture-consultation.nri.org/summaries/wp13.pdf.

Aistara, Guntra. 2011. "Seeds of Kin, Kin of Seeds: The Commodification of Organic Seeds and Social Relations in Costa Rica and Latvia." *Ethnography* 12, no. 4: 490–517.

Appadurai, Arjun. 1990. "Disjuncture and Difference in the Global Cultural Economy." *Public Culture* 2, no. 2: 1–24.

Appelbaum, Richard P., William L. F. Felstiner, and Volkmar Gessner. 2001. *Rules and Networks: The Legal Culture of Global Business Transactions.* Oxford, England: Hart.

Arete–Research & Consulting in Economics. n.d. "Inventory of Certification Schemes for Agricultural Products and Foodstuffs Marketed in the EU Member States." http://ec.europa.eu/agriculture/quality/certification/inventory/inventory-data -aggregations_en.pdf.

A Szólás Szabadsága (Freedom of Speech) [Television Program]. 2004. October 29. No longer online.

ATV. 2011. "MAL: nem a cég tevékenysége okozta a vörösiszap-katasztrófát" (MAL: The company's activities were not the cause of the red mud catastrophe). December 27. http://atv.hu/belfold/20111227_mal_nem_a_ceg_tevekenysege_okozta_a _vorosiszap_katasztrofat.

Bánvölgyi, György, and Tran Minh Huan. n.d. "De-watering, Disposal and Utilization of Red Mud: State of the Art and Emerging Technologies." http://www.redmud .org/Files/banvolgyi040110.pdf.

Barber, Dan. 2008. "Dan Barber's foie gras parable." Talk at Taste3 Conference. TED video. 20:19. http://www.ted.com/talks/lang/en/dan_barber_s_surprising_foie _gras_parable.html.

Barroso, Manuel. 2013. "State of the Union address 2013." European Commission— SPEECH/13/684. http://europa.eu/rapid/press-release_SPEECH-13-684_en.htm.

Barry, Andrew. 2001. *Political Machines: Governing a Technological Society.* London: Continuum.

Bartley, Tim. 2014. "Rules: Global Production and the Puzzle of Rules." In *Framing the Global: Entry Points for Research,* edited by Hilary Kahn, 229–52. Bloomington: Indiana University Press.

BBC. 2003. "EU growth sparks food fears." January 15. news.bbc.co.uk/2/hi/uk_news /2659829.stm.

Beck, Ulrich. 1992. *Risk Society: Towards a New Modernity.* London: Sage.

Bennett, Jane. 2010. *Vibrant Matter: A Political Ecology of Things.* Durham, N.C.: Duke University Press.

Berdahl, Daphne. 1999. *Where the World Ended: Re-Unification and Identity in the German Borderland.* Berkeley: University of California Press.

Berend, Ivan T., and György Ránki. 1985. *The Hungarian Economy in the Twentieth Century.* London: Croom Helm.

Bessenyey-Williams, Margit. 2001. "Exporting the Democratic Deficit: Hungary's Experience with the EU Integration." *Problems of Post-Communism* 48, no. 1: 27–38.

Bingen, Jim, and Lawrence Busch, eds. 2006. *Agricultural Standards: The Shape of the Global Food And Fiber System.* Dordrecht, the Netherlands: Springer.

Binnemans, Koen, Yiannis Pontikes, Peter Tom Jones, Tom Van Gerven, and Bart Blanpain. 2013. "Recovery of Rare Earths From Industrial Waste Residues: A Concise Review." Proceedings of the 3rd International Slag Valorisation Symposium: the Transition to Sustainable Materials Management. 191–205.

Bockman, Johanna. 2011. *Markets in the Name of Socialism: The Left-Wing Origins of Neoliberalism.* Stanford, Calif.: Stanford University Press.

Bodnár, Judit. 2001. *Fin-de-Millénaire Budapest: Metamorphoses of Urban Life.* Minneapolis: University of Minnesota Press.

de Bois, Robin. 2010. "Red Mud in Hungary: A Predictable, International and Major Disaster." http://www.robindesbois.org/english/risk/red_mud_hungary.html.

Bonne, R., N. Wright, L. Camberou, and F. Boccas. 2005. "Guidelines on HACCP, GMP, and GHP for Asean food SMEs." EC-ASEAN Economic Cooperation Programme on Standards, Quality & Conformity Assessment. Asia/2003/069–236. The European Union and the ASEAN. http://ec.europa.eu/food/training/haccp_en.pdf.

Borhi, Laszlo G. 2000. *The Merchants of the Kremlin: The Economic Roots of Soviet Expansion in Hungary.* Working Paper No. 28. Washington, D.C.: Woodrow Wilson International Center For Scholars.

Böröcz, József. 1992. "Dual Dependency and Property Vacuum: Social Change on the State Socialist Semiperiphery." *Theory and Society* 21: 77–104.

———. 1993. "Simulating the Great Transformation: Property Change under Prolonged Informality in Hungary." *Archives européennes de sociologie/Europäisches Archiv für Soziologie/European Archives for Sociology* XXXIV: 81–107.

———. 2000. "The Fox and the Raven: The European Union and Hungary Renegotiate the Margins of Europe." *Comparative Studies in History and Society* 42, no. 4: 847–75.

———. 2001. "Introduction: Empire and Coloniality in the 'Eastern Enlargement' of the European Union." In *Empire's New Clothes: Unveiling EU-Enlargement,* edited by József Böröcz and Melinda Kovács, 4–50. Telford, U.K.: Central Europe Review e-books.

———. 2010. *The European Union and Global Social Change: A Critical Geopolitical-Economic Analysis.* Abingdon, Oxford, U.K.: Routledge.

Braudel, Fernand. 1981. *The Structures of Everyday Life: Civilization and Capitalism 15th–18th Century. Vol. 1.* New York: Harper and Row.

Braun, Bruce, and Sarah J. Whatmore, eds. 2010. *Political Matter: Technoscience, Democracy and Public Life.* Minneapolis: University of Minnesota Press.

Brown, Oli. 2005. *Supermarket Buying Power, Global Commodity Chains and Smallholder Farmers in the Developing World.* Human Development Report Office Occasional Paper 2005/4. New York: U.N. Development Programme. http://hdr.undp.org/en /reports/global/hdr2005/papers/HDR2005_Brown_Oli_41.pdf.

Brown, Oli, and Christina Sander. 2007. *Supermarket Buying Power: Global Supply Chains and Smallholder Farmers.* Winnipeg, Canada: International Institute for Sustainable Development. http://www.iisd.org/publications/pub.aspx?pno=851.

Brunsson Nils, Jacobsson Bengt, and associates. 2000. *A World of Standards.* Oxford, UK: Oxford University Press.

Budapest Analyses. 2004. "The state of Hungarian agriculture on the eve of accession to the European Union." http://bpfrakcio.hu/ba/english/budapestanalyses_41_en .html.

Bunce, Valerie. 1995. "Should Transitologists be Grounded?" *Slavic Review* 54, no. 1: 111–27.

———. 1999. "Ten Years After 1989: What Have We Learned?" *Slavic Review* 58, no. 4: 756–93.

Burawoy, Michael. 1991. "Reconstructing Social Theories." In *Ethnography Unbound: Power and Resistance in the Modern Metropolis,* edited by Michael Burawoy. Berkeley: University of California Press.

Burawoy, Michael, Joseph A. Blum, Sheba George, Zsuzsa Gille, Teresa Gowan, Lynne Haney, Maren Klawiter, Steven H. Lopez, Seán Ó Riain, and Millie Thayer. 2000. *Global Ethnography: Forces, Connections and Imaginations in a Postmodern World.* Berkeley: University of California Press.

Burawoy, Michael, and János Lukács. 1992. *Ideology and Reality in Hungary's Road To Capitalism.* Chicago: University of Chicago Press.

Busch, Lawrence. 2000. "The Moral Economy of Grades and Standards." *Journal of Rural Studies* 16: 273–83.

———. 2004. "Grades and Standards in the Social Construction of Safe Food." In *The Politics of Food,* edited by Marianne Elisabeth Lien and Brigitte Nerlich, 163–78. New York: Berg.

Caro, Mark. 2009. *The Foie Gras Wars: How a 5,000-year-old Delicacy Inspired the World's Fiercest Food Fight.* New York: Simon & Schuster.

Casals, Felipe García [Pavel Campeanu]. 1980. *The Syncretic Society.* White Plains, N.Y.: M. E. Sharpe.

Castells, Manuel. 1989. "Conclusion: The Reconstruction of Social Meaning in the Space of Flows." In *The Informational City,* 348–53. Oxford, U.K.: Blackwell.

———. 1997. *The Power of Identity. The Information Age: Economy, Society and Culture*, vol. 2. Malden, Mass.: Blackwell.

Castree, Noel. 2002. "False Antitheses? Marxism, Nature and Actor-Networks." *Antipode* 34: 119–48.

Chalmers, Damian, and Mariana Chaves. 2014. "Union Democratic Overload and the Unloading of European Democracy Before and After the Crisis." In *Democratic Politics in a European Union Under Stress*, edited by Olaf Cramme and Sara Hobolt, 155–79. Oxford, UK: Oxford University Press.

Chander, Anupam, and Madhavi Sunder. 2004. "The Romance of the Public Domain." *California Law Review* 92: 1331–1373.

CIA Office of Current Intelligence. 1952. "Current Intelligence Bulletin." June 20. Radio Free Europe Archives.

Cidell, Julie L., and Heike C. Alberts. 2006. "Constructing Quality: The Multinational Histories of Chocolate." *Geoforum* 37, no. 6: 999–1007.

Codron, Jean-Marie, Eric Giraud-Héraud, and Louis-Georges Soler. 2005. "Minimum Quality Standards, Premium Private Labels, and European Meat and Fresh Produce Retailing." *Food Policy* 30, no. 3: 270–83.

Coe, Neil M., and Martin Hess. 2005. "The Internationalization of Retailing: Implications for Supply Network Restructuring in East Asia and Eastern Europe." *Journal of Economic Geography* 5, no. 4: 449–73.

Collins, K. 1996. "Bovine spongiform encephalopathy (BSE) – (Creutzfeldt-Jakob Disease) CJD: Our Health at Risk?" *European Parliament*, Hearing No. 17. Brussels.

Comaroff, Jean and John. 2009. *Ethnicity, Inc.* Chicago: University of Chicago Press.

Cooke, Bill, and Uma Kothari, eds. 2001. *Participation: The New Tyranny?* London: Zed Books.

Coole, Diana, and Samantha Frost. 2010. "Introducing the New Materialisms. In *New Materialisms: Ontology, Agency, and Politics*, edited by Diana Coole and Samantha Frost, 1–43. Durham, N.C.: Duke University Press.

Cooling, David J. 2007. "Improving the Sustainability of Residue Management Practices—AlcoaWorld Alumina Australia." In *Paste 2007. Proceedings of the Tenth International Seminar on Paste and Thickened Tailings*, edited by A. Fourie and R. J. Jewell. Perth: Australian Centre for Geomechanics. http://www.acg.uwa.edu.au/__data /page/4096/Cooling2.pdf.

Creed, Gerald. 1999. "Deconstructing Socialism in Bulgaria." In *Uncertain Transition: Ethnographies of Change in the Postsocialist World*, edited by Michael Burawoy and Katherine Verdery, 223–44. Lanham, Md.: Rowman & Littlefield.

———. 2010. *Masquerade and Postsocialism: Ritual and Cultural Dispossession in Bulgaria*. Bloomington: Indiana University Press.

Cronon, William. 1991. *Nature's Metropolis: Chicago and the Great West*. New York: W. W. Norton.

Czakó, Ágnes, Tibor Kuczi, György Lengyel, and Ágnes Vajda. 1995. "A kisvállalkozások néhány jellemzője a kilencvenes évek elején" (Some characteristics of small enterprises at the beginning of the '90s). *Közgazdasági Szemle* 42, no. 4: 399–419.

Dant, Tim. 2006. "Material Civilization: Things and Society." *The British Journal of Sociology* 57, no. 2: 289–308.

DeSoucey, Michaela. 2010. "Gastronationalism: Food Traditions and Authenticity Politics in the European Union." *American Sociological Review* 75, no. 3: 432–55.

Dryzek, John S. 1997. *The Politics of the Earth: Environmental Discourses.* Oxford: Oxford University Press.

Dunn, Elizabeth C. 2003. "Trojan Pig: Paradoxes of Food Safety Regulation." *Environment and Planning A* 35, no. 8: 1493–1511.

———. 2004. *Privatizing Poland: Baby Food, Big Business, and the Remaking of Labor.* Ithaca, N.Y.: Cornell University Press.

———. 2005. "Standards and Person-Making in East Central Europe." In *Global Assemblages: Technology, Politics, and Ethics as Anthropological Problems*, edited by Aihwa Ong and Stephen J. Collier, 173–94. Malden, Mass.: Blackwell.

———. 2007. "Escherichia Coli, Corporate Discipline and the Failure of the Sewer State." *Space and Polity* 11, no. 1: 35–53.

Earth Times. 2011. "EU: Hungary Classified Red Mud Reservoir Incorrectly – Summary." http://www.earthtimes.org/articles/news/362230,reservoir-incorrectly-summary.html.

Élelmiszeripari Gazdaságtan Tanszék (Department of Food Economics). 2009. *A libamáj, mint örökség, gazdasági ágazat és termék: Fogyasztói kutatás a hazai hízottmáj-ágazattal kapcsolatban* (Foie gras as heritage, economic sector, and product: Consumer survey on the domestic foie gras sector). Budapest: Budapesti Corvinus Egyetem, Élelmiszertudományi Kar.

Esbenshade, Richard S. 2006. "The Populist-Urbanist Debate in Hungary and the Divided Construction of Hungarian National Identity, 1929–1944." PhD diss. University of California, Santa Cruz.

European Aluminum Association. 2013. *Sustainable Development Indicators for the Aluminum Industry in Europe: 2012 Key Facts and Figures.* Brussels. http://www.alueurope.eu/wp-content/uploads/2011/09/EAA-sustainabilty-leaflet_optimal_site_January 2014.pdf.

European Commission. 1993. European Council in Copenhagen—21–22 June 1993—Conclusions of the Presidency—European Council—DOC/93/3 22/06/1993. http://europa.eu/rapid/press-release_DOC-93-3_en.htm.

———. 2003. "EU Enlargement: Questions and Answers on Food Safety Issues." Memo /03/88. December 5. Brussels. http://europa.eu/rapid/press-release_MEMO-03-88_en.htm?locale=en.

———. 2010. "European Commission Communication—EU Best Practice Guidelines for Voluntary Certification Schemes for Agricultural Products and Foodstuffs." *Official Journal of the European Union.* December 16. C 341/5. http://eur-lex.europa.eu/legal-content/en/ALL/?uri=CELEX:52010XC1216(02).

———. 2011. "Other Acts: European Commission." *Official Journal of the European Union.* October 14. C 303/16–20.

———. n.d. Agriculture and Rural Development. Agriculture and Food. DOOR. http://ec.europa.eu/agriculture/quality/door/list.html.

European Commission Directorate for Agriculture. 1998. "Agricultural Situation and Perspectives in the Central and Eastern European Countries." http://ec.europa.eu/agriculture/publi/peco/hungary/summary/sum_en.htm.

————. 2002. "Analysis of the Impact on Agricultural Markets and Incomes of EU Enlargement to the CEECS." http://ec.europa.eu/agriculture/publi/reports/ceec impact/sum_en.pdf.

European Commission, Directorate-General for Research and Innovation. 2007. *European Research on Traditional Foods.* Brussels: European Commission Community Research.

Evans, Peter, B. 1997. *State-Society Synergy: Government and Social Capital in Development.* Berkeley: University of California International and Area Studies.

Farmer, Erica A. 2014. "Codifying Consensus and Constructing Boundaries: Setting the Limits of Appellation d'origine contrôlée Protection in Bordeaux, France." *PoLAR: Political and Legal Anthropology Review* 37, no. 1: 126–44.

Fehér, Ferenc, Ágnes Heller, and György Márkus. 1983. *Dictatorship Over Needs.* New York: St. Martin's Press.

Fehérváry, Krisztina. 2013. *Politics in Color and Concrete: Socialist Materialities and the Middle Class in Hungary.* Bloomington: Indiana University Press.

Fine, Ben. 2005. "From Actor-Network Theory to Political Economy." *Capitalism, Nature, Socialism* 16, no. 4: 91–108, 149.

Földvári, Zsuzsa. 2009. "Jürgen Faulmann állatjogi harcos: 'Nem tárgyalunk, folytatjuk a kampányt'" (Jürgen Faulmann, fighter for animal rights: "We don't negotiate, we continue the campaign"). *HVG.* January 14, 22–23. http://hvg.hu/hvgfriss/2009.03 /200903_Jurgen_Faulmann_allatjogi_harcos_Nem_targya.

Foster, John Bellamy. 1999. "Marx's Theory of Metabolic Rift: Classical Foundations for Environmental Sociology." *AJS* 105, no. 2: 366–405.

————. 2000. *Marx's Ecology: Materialism and Nature.* New York: Monthly Review Press.

Foucault, Michel. 1977. *Discipline and Punish: The Birth of the Prison.* Translated by Alan Sheridan. New York: Vintage Press.

————. 2003. *Society Must Be Defended: Lectures at the Collège de France, 1975–1976.* Translated by David Macey. New York: St. Martin's Press.

————. 2010. *The Birth of Biopolitics: Lectures at the Collège de France, 1978–1979.* Translated by Graham Burchell. New York: Picador.

Four Paws (FP) Press Release. 2008. "A Minisztérium elárulja a Magyar baromfi ipari dolgozókat és az állatokat" (The ministry is betraying the workers in the Hungarian poultry industry and the animals). No longer available online.

Fraser, Nancy. 1997. *Justice Interruptus: Critical Reflections on the "Postsocialist" Condition.* New York: Routledge.

————. 2013. "A Triple Movement? Parsing the Politics of Crisis after Polanyi." *New Left Review* 81: 119–32.

Fraser, Nancy, and Axel Honneth. 2003. *Redistribution or Recognition? A Political-Philosophical Exchange.* London: Verso.

Freidberg, Susanne. 2004. *French Beans and Food Scares: Culture and Commerce in an Anxious Age.* New York: Oxford University Press.

Fulponi, Linda. 2006. "Private Voluntary Standards in the Food System: The Perspective of Major Food Retailers in OECD Countries." *Food Policy* 31, no. 1: 1–13.

Gareau, Brian. 2005. "We Have Never Been Human: Agential Nature, ANT, and Marxist Political Ecology." *Capitalism Nature Socialism* 16, no. 4: 127–40.

Garsten, Christina, and Kerstin Jacobsson. 2011. "Post-Political Regulation: Soft Power and Post-Political Visions in Global Governance." *Critical Sociology* 39, no. 3: 421–37.

Geismar, Haidy. 2011. "'Material Culture Studies' and Other Ways to Theorize Objects: A Primer to a Regional Debate." *Comparative Studies in Society and History* 53, no. 1: 210–18.

Gereffi, Gary, Ronie Garcia-Johnson, and Erika Sasser. 2001. "The NGO-Industrial Complex." *Foreign Policy* 125, no. 4: 56–65.

Ghodsee, Kristen. 2011. *Lost in Transition: Ethnographies of Everyday Life after Communism.* Durham, N.C.: Duke University Press.

Gille, Zsuzsa. 2006. "Detached Flows or Grounded Place-Making Projects?" In *Governing Environmental Flows: Global Challenges to Social Theory*, edited by Arthur P. J. Mol and Gert Spaargaren, 137–56. Cambridge, Mass.: MIT Press.

———. 2007. *From the Cult of Waste to the Trash Heap of History: The Politics of Waste in Socialist and Postsocialist Hungary.* Bloomington: Indiana University Press.

———. 2010. "Is There a Global Postsocialist Condition?" *Global Society* 24, no. 1: 9–30.

———. 2013. "From Risk to Waste: Global Food Waste Regimes." In *Waste Matters: New Perspectives on Food and Society. The Sociological Review* Monograph Series, vol. 60, edited by David Evans, Hugh Campbell, and Anne Murcott, 27–46. Malden, Mass.: Wiley-Blackwell.

Gille, Zsuzsa, and Sean O'Riain. 2002. "Global Ethnography." *Annual Review of Sociology* 28: 271–95.

Government Office for Science. 2011. *Expert Forum on the Reduction of Food Waste: 'How Can Waste Reduction Help to Healthily and Sustainably Feed a Future Global Population of Nine Billion People?'* Workshop Report, Organised by the UK Science and Innovation Network in collaboration with Foresight, 23–24 February 2010, The Rubens Hotel, London. http://www.bis.gov.uk/assets/bispartners/foresight/docs /food-and-farming/workshops/11-608-w4-expert-forum-reduction-of-food-waste.

Greenberg, Russell, and Peter P. Marra. 2005. *Birds of Two Worlds: The Ecology and Evolution of Migration.* Baltimore: Johns Hopkins University Press.

Greenpeace. 2010. "Jóval mérgezőbb az iszap, mint a hivatalos tájékoztatás elmondta" (The sludge is much more toxic than stated by official information). http://green peace.hu/kereses/p1/t272.

Haas, Peter M. 1992. "Introduction: Epistemic Communities and International Policy Coordination." *International Organization* 46, no. 1: 1–35.

Habermas, Jürgen. 1970. *Toward a Rational Society: Student Protest, Science, and Politics.* Translated by Jeremy J. Shapiro. Boston: Beacon Press.

Hajer, Maarten. 1995. *The Politics of Environmental Discourse: Ecological Modernization and the Policy Process.* Oxford, U.K.: Clarendon Press.

Halász, Zoltán. 1987. *Kis magyar paprikakönyv* (Little Hungarian book of paprika). Budapest: Corvina.

Hankiss, Elemér. 1984. "Második Társadalom? Kísérlet egy fogalom meghatározására és egy valóságtartalom leírására." (Second Society? An attempt to define a concept and to describe a reality content). *Valóság* 27, no. 11: 25–44.

———. 1990. *East European Alternatives.* New York: Oxford University Press.

Hart, Gillian. 2002. *Disabling Globalization: Places of Power in Post-Apartheid South Africa*. Berkeley: University of California Press.

Harvey, David. 1990. *The Condition of Postmodernity: An Inquiry into the Origins of Cultural Change*. Oxford, U.K.: Blackwell.

Hatanaka, Maki, and Jason Konefal. 2013. "Legitimacy and Standard Development in Multi-stakeholder Initiatives: A Case Study of the Leonardo Academy's Sustainable Agriculture Standard Initiative." *International Journal of Sociology of Agriculture and Food* 20, no. 2: 155–73.

Havel, Vaclav. 1996. "Europe as Task." Speech given in Aachen, Germany. May 15. http://www.pro-europa.eu/index.php?option=com_content&view=article&id=27:vaclav-havel-europe-as-task&catid=11:the-struggle-for-the-union-of-europe&Itemid=17.

Health and Medicine Week. 2004. "Hungarian Government Bans Sale of Paprika." November 15: 433.

Heath, Deborah, and Anne Meneley. 2010. "The Naturecultures of Foie Gras: Techniques of the Body and a Contested Ethics of Care." *Food, Culture and Society* 13, no. 3: 421–52.

Henson, Spencer, and Thomas Reardon. 2005. "Private Agri-Food Standards: Implications for Food Policy and the Agri-Food System." *Food Policy* 30, no. 3: 241–53.

Hetherington, Kevin. 2004. "Secondhandedness: Consumption, Disposal, and Absent Presence." *Environment and Planning D: Society and Space*. 22, no. 1: 157–73.

Hodúr, Cecilia, Zsuzsanna László, and Zsuzsa Hovorka Horváth. 2010. "A Ban on Paprika in Hungary." In *Case Studies in Food Safety and Environmental Health*, edited by Peter Ho and Margarida Vieira, 53–56. *Integrating Safety and Environmental Knowledge Into Food Studies towards European Sustainable Development*, vol. 6. New York: Springer.

Holland, Dorothy C., William Lachicotte, Debra Skinner, and Carole Cain. 1998. *Identity and Agency in Cultural Worlds*. Cambridge, Mass.: Harvard University Press.

Humphrey, Caroline. 1991. "'Icebergs,' Barter, and the Mafia in Provincial Russia. *Anthropology Today* 7, no. 2: 8–13.

———. 1999. "Traders, 'Disorder,' Citizenship Regimes in Provincial Russia." In *Uncertain Transition: Ethnographies of Change in the Postsocialist World*, edited by Michael Burawoy and Katherine Verdery, 19–52. Lanham, Md.: Rowman & Littlefield.

HVG. 2004. "Malomparádé (Mill Circus). November 6: 95.

———. 2010. "MAL-vezér: a vörösiszap nem mérgező, persze fürdeni nem kell benne" (Head of MAL: "The red mud is not poisonous, of course one wouldn't want to bathe in it"). October 5. http://hvg.hu/itthon/20101005_iszapomles_mal.

Index. 2004. "Egy éve parlamenti téma volt az import paprika" (A year ago the Parliament was discussing import paprika). October 28. http://index.hu/gazdasag/magyar/pappar104102/.

———. 2005. "1–2 tonna mérgezett paprika kerülhetett a fogyasztókhoz" (One to two tons of contaminated paprika may have reached consumers). February 26. http://index.hu/gazdasag/magyar/papo50225/.

Jávor, Benedek, and Miklós Hargitai, eds. 2011. *Kolontár-jelentés: A vörösiszap-baleset okai és tanulságai* (Kolontár report: Causes and lessons from the red mud disaster). Budapest: Greens/European Free Alliance Parliamentary Group in the European Parliament and LMP Party.

Jones, B. E. H., and R. J. Haynes. 2011. "Bauxite Processing Residue: A Critical Review of Its Formation, Properties, Storage, and Revegetation." *Critical Reviews in Environmental Science and Technology* 41, no. 3: 271–315.

Juhász, Ádám. 1977. "Development of the Aluminium Industry in Hungary." *Acta Oeconomica* 18, no. 3/4: 355–69.

Juntti, Meri. 2012. "Implementing Cross Compliance for Agriculture in the EU: Relational Agency, Power and Action in Different Socio-Material Contexts." *Sociologia Ruralis* 52, no. 3: 294–310.

Kapoor, Ilan. 2005. "Participatory Development, Complicity and Desire." *Third World Quarterly* 26, no. 8: 1203–1220.

Kehagia, Fotini. 2008. "A Successful Pilot Project Demonstrating the Re-use Potential of Bauxite Residue in Embankment Construction." *Resources, Conservation and Recycling* 54, no. 7: 417–21.

Kennedy, Michael D. 2002. *Cultural Formations of Postcommunism: Emancipation, Transition, Nation and War.* Minneapolis: University of Minnesota Press.

Kennedy, Michael D., and Pauline Gianoplus. 1994. "Entrepreneurs and Expertise: A Cultural Encounter in the Making of Post-Communist Capitalism in Poland." *East European Politics and Societies* 8, no. 1: 58–93.

Kimura, Aya Hirata. 2013. "Standards as Hybrid Forum: Comparison of the Post-Fukushima Radiation Standards by a Consumer Cooperative, the Private Sector, and the Japanese Government." *International Journal of Sociology of Agriculture and Food* 20, no. 1: 11–29.

Kiss, Judit. 2001. "The Agricultural Aspects of Hungarian Accession to the EU." Institute for World Economics, Hungarian Academy of Sciences. http://mek.oszk.hu/03800/03811/03811.pdf.

Kocsubé, Sándor, János Varga, Gyöngyi Szigeti, Nikolett Baranyi, Katalin Suri, Beáta Tóth, Éva Toldi, Tibor Bartók, and Akos Mesterházy. 2013. "Aspergillus Species as Mycotoxin Producers in Agricultural Products in Central Europe." Матице српске за природне науке / *Jour. Nat. Sci, Matica Srpska Novi Sad* 124: 13–25.

Kornai, János. 1980. *Economics of Shortage.* Amsterdam: North-Holland.

———. 1990. "The Affinity Between Ownership Forms and Coordination Mechanisms: The Common Experience of Reform in Socialist Countries." *Journal of Economic Perspectives* 4, no. 3: 131–47.

KSH. 2013. "Total Production of Harvested Vegetables and Hungarian Red Paprika (2000–2012)." https://www.ksh.hu/docs/eng/xstadat/xstadat_annual/i_omn023a.html?3351.

Kundera, Milan. 1984. "The Tragedy of Central Europe." *New York Review of Books* 31, no. 7: 33–38.

Lampland, Martha, and Susan Leigh Star, eds. 2009. *Standards and Their Stories: How Quantifying, Classifying and Formalizing Practices Shape Everyday Life.* Ithaca, N.Y.: Cornell University Press.

Latour, Bruno. 1993a. [1991]. *We Have Never Been Modern.* Translated by Catherine Porter. Cambridge, Mass.: Harvard University Press.

———. 1993b. [1984] *The Pasteurization of France.* Translated by Alan Sheridan and John Law. Cambridge, Mass.: Harvard University Press.

———. 1994. "On Technical Mediation—Philosophy, Sociology, Genealogy." *Common Knowledge* 3, no. 2: 29–64.

———. 2002. "Morality and Technology: The End of the Means." *Theory, Culture & Society* 19, no. 5/6: 247–60.

———. 2005. *Reassembling the Social: An Introduction to Actor-Network Theory*. Oxford: Oxford University Press.

Law, John. 2004. "And If the Global Were Small and Noncoherent? Method, Complexity, and the Baroque." *Environment and Planning D: Society and Space* 22: 13–26.

———. 2007. "Actor Network Theory and Material Semiotics." Manuscript. Version of April 25, 2007. http://www.heterogeneities.net/publications/Law-ANTand MaterialSemiotics.pdf.

Lengyel, György. 2012. *Potential Entrepreneurs: Entrepreneurial Inclination in Hungary, 1988–2011*. Manuscript. Budapest.

Lipschutz, Ronnie, D., with Judith Mayer. 1996. *Global Civil Society and Global Environmental Governance: The Politics of Nature from Place to Planet*. Albany: State University of New York Press.

Loeber, Anne, Maarten Hajer, and Les Levidow. 2011. "Agro-food Crises: Institutional and Discursive Changes in the Food Scares Era." *Science as Culture* 20, no. 2: 147–55.

London Economics. 2008. Evaluation of the CAP policy on protected designations of origin (PDO) and protected geographical indications (PGI) final report. http:// ec.europa.eu/agriculture/eval/reports/pdopgi/report_en.pdf.

Lotti, Ariane. 2010. "The Commoditization of Products and Taste: Slow Food and the Conservation of Agrobiodiversity." *Agriculture and Human Values* 27: 71–83.

Lyon, Sarah, and Mark Moberg. 2010. *Fair Trade and Social Justice: Global Ethnographies*. New York: New York University Press.

MacKenzie, Donald. 1984. "Marx and the Machine." *Technology and Culture* 25, no. 3: 473–502.

Mandel, Ernest. 1974. "Ten Theses on the Social and Economic Laws Governing the Society Transitional Between Capitalism and Socialism." Translated by Iain L. Fraser. *Critique* 3: 5–21.

Marcuse, Herbert. 1964. *One-Dimensional Man: Studies in the Ideology of Advanced Industrial Society*. Boston: Beacon Press.

Marody, Mira, and Anna Giza-Poleszczuk. 2000. "Changing Images of Identity in Poland: From the Self-Sacrificing to the Self-Investing Woman." In *Reproducing Gender: Politics, Publics, and Everyday Life after Socialism*, edited by Susan Gal and Gail Kligman, 151–75. Princeton, N.J.: Princeton University Press.

Marres, Noortje. 2012. *Material Participation: Technology, the Environment and Everyday Publics*. Basingstoke, U.K.: Palgrave Macmillan.

Massey Doreen. 1994. *Space, Place and Gender*. Minneapolis: University of Minnesota Press.

Mayes, Will M., Adam P. Jarvis, Ian T. Burke, Melanie Walton, and Katalin Gruiz. 2011. "Trace and Rare Earth Element Dispersal Downstream of the Ajka Red Mud Spill, Hungary." In *11th International Mine Water Association Congress–Mine Water–*

Managing the Challenges, edited by Rüde, Freund, and Wolkersdorfer, 29–34. Aachen, Germany: International Mine Water Association.

McMichael, Philip. 1996. "Globalization: Myths and Realities." *Rural Sociology* 61, no. 1: 25–55.

Miller, Daniel. 2002. *Material Cultures: Why Some Things Matter.* London: Taylor & Francis.

Mincyte, Diana. 2011. "Subsistence and Sustainability in Post-Industrial Europe: The Politics of Small-Scale Farming in Europeanizing Lithuania." *Sociologia Ruralis* 51, no. 2: 101–18.

———. 2012. "How Milk Does the World Good: Vernacular Sustainability and Alternative Food Systems in Post-Socialist Europe." *Agriculture and Human Values* 29, no. 1: 41–52.

Ministry of Agriculture and Rural Development. 2007. *"New Hungary" Rural Development Programme, 2007–2013.* http://www.termeszetvedelem.hu/_user/downloads /ett/new_hungary_rural_development_programme_official_20092007.pdf.

Mintz, Sidney. 1986. *Sweetness and Power: The Place of Sugar in Modern History.* New York: Penguin.

Mitchell, Timothy. 2002. *Rule of Experts: Egypt, Techno-Politics, Modernity.* Berkeley: University of California Press.

———. 2009. "Carbon Democracy." *Economy and Society* 38, no. 3: 399–432.

Mol, Arthur P. J. 1995. *The Refinement of Production: Ecological Modernization Theory and the Chemical Industry.* Utrecht, the Netherlands: Van Arkel.

Morgan, Kevin, Terry Marsden, and Jonathan Murdoch. 2006. *Worlds of Food: Place, Power, and Provenance in the Food Chain.* Oxford: Oxford University Press.

Moss, David. 2004. "Is Good Policy Unimplementable? Reflections on the Ethnography of Aid Policy and Practice." *Development and Change* 35, no. 4: 639–71.

MTA (Magyar Tudományos Akadémia [Hungarian Academy of Sciences]). 2010. *Tájékoztató a kolontári vörösiszap tározó környezetében végzett vizsgálatokról* (Information about the tests performed in the vicinity of the Kolontár red mud impoundment). http://mta.hu/mta_hirei/tajekoztato-a-kolontari-vorosiszap-tarozo -kornyezeteben-vegzett-vizsgalatokrol-125761.

MTI (Magyar Távirati Iroda [Hungarian News Agency]). 2006. "A Forrás Vagyonkezelési és Befektetési Rt. értékesítette a Szegedi Paprika Fűszer- és Konzervgyártó ZRt.-ben meglévő 66,67 százalékos részesedését a sükösdi székhelyű Házi Piros Paprika Kft.-nek – tájékoztattak az érintett cégek" (The Forrás Wealth Management and Investment Company, Inc. sold its 66.67% share in the Szegedi Paprika Spice and Canning Company, Ltd. to Házi Piros Paprika, LLC—the companies involved reported). February 8.

Mueller, Tom. 2011. *Extra Virginity: The Sublime and Scandalous World of Olive Oil.* London: Atlantic.

Mukerji, Chandra. 2010. "The Territorial State as a Figured World of Power: Strategics, Logistics, and Impersonal Rule." *Sociological Theory* 28, no. 4: 402–24.

Nally, David. 2011. "The Biopolitics of Food Provisioning." *Transactions of the Institute of British Geographers* 36, no. 1: 37–53.

National Development Agency. 2005. *A Nemzeti Fejlesztési Terv szerepe az ajkai kistérség fejlődésében: Kistérségi esettanulmány* (The role of the National Development Plan in the development of the Ajka local region: Case study of a local region). palyazat.gov .hu/download/928/Ajka.doc.

National Waste Management Plan [of Hungary]. 2003–2008. http://www.kvvm.hu /szakmai/hulladekgazd/oht_ang.htm.

Nederveen Pieterse, Jan. 2002. "Globalization as Reworking Borders: Hierarchical Integration and New Border Theory." Paper presented at the International Sociological Association conference, New Orleans, La., March.

Noble, David. F. 1984. *Forces of Production: A Social History of Machine Tool Automation.* New York: Alfred A. Knopf.

OECD. 2003. "Voluntary Approaches for Environmental Policy Effectiveness, Efficiency and Usage in Policy Mixes." http://www.keepeek.com/Digital-Asset-Management /oecd/environment/voluntary-approaches-for-environmental-policy_9789264 101784-en.

Ong, Aihwa, and Stephen J. Collier, eds. 2005. *Global Assemblages: Technology, Politics, and Ethics as Anthropological Problems.* Malden, Mass.: Blackwell.

Paramguru, R. K., P. C. Rath, and V. N. Misra. 2005. "Trends in Red Mud Utilization— A Review." *Mineral Processing and Extractive Metallurgy* 26, no. 1: 1–29.

Paul, Katharina T. 2012. "The Europeanization of Food Safety: A Discourse-Analytical Approach." *Journal of European Public Policy* 19, no. 4: 549–66.

Peck, Jamie. 2013. "Explaining (with) Neoliberalism." *Territory, Politics, Governance* 1, no. 2: 132–57.

Perlez, Jane. 1994. "Budapest Journal: Crisis of Goulash Capitalism: Where's the Paprika?" *The New York Times.* October 11.

Pickering, Andrew. 1995. *The Mangle of Practice: Time, Agency, and Science.* Chicago: University of Chicago Press.

———. 2001. "Practice and Posthumanism: Social Theory and a History of Agency." In *The Practice Turn in Contemporary Theory*, edited by Theodore R. Schatzki, Karin Knorr Certina, and Eike von Savigny, 163–74. London: Routledge.

Pimbert, Michel P., John Thompson, and William T. Vorley, with Tom Fox, Nazneen Kanji, N. and Cecilia Tacoli. 2001. *Global Restructuring, Agri-Food Systems and Livelihood.* Gatekeeper Series no. 100. London: International Institute for Environment and Development.

Polanyi, Karl. 1944. *The Great Transformation: The Political Economy and the Origins of Our Time.* Beacon Hill, Mass.: Beacon Hill Press.

Pollan, Michael. 2006. *The Omnivore's Dilemma: A Natural History of Four Meals.* New York: Penguin.

Potočnik, Janez. 2011. "EU Commissioner for Environment: Industrial Disasters can be Prevented by Better Implementation of EU Law." 2011 Civic Seminar in the Shadow of Industrial Catastrophe. European Commission—SPEECH/11/325 06 /05/2011 Budapest. May 6. http://europa.eu/rapid/press-release_SPEECH-11-325 _en.htm.

Power, Greg, Markus Gräfe, and Craig Klauber. 2009. "Review of Current Bauxite Residue Management, Disposal and Storage: Practices, Engineering and Science."

CSIRO Document DMR3608. http://www.asiapacificpartnership.org/pdf/Projects /Aluminium/Review%2520of%2520Current%2520Bauxite%2520Residue%2520 Management%2520Disposal%2520Storage_Aug09_sec.pdf.

Rapid Alert System for Food and Feed (RASFF)—Introduction. n.d. http://ec.europa .eu/food/food/rapidalert/reports/.

Red Mud Project. n.d. "Red Mud Disposal." http://www.redmud.org/Disposal.html.

Rose, Nikolas. 1999. *Powers of Freedom: Reframing Political Thought.* Cambridge: Cambridge University Press.

Rudy, Alan P. 2005. "On ANT and Relational Materialisms." *Capitalism Nature Socialism* 16, no. 4: 109–25.

Sampson, Steven. 2002. "Beyond Transition: Rethinking Elite Configurations in the Balkans." In *Postsocialism: Ideals, Ideologies and Practices in Eurasia*, edited by C. M. Hann, 297–316. London: Routledge.

Sassen, Saskia. 1995. "The State and The Global City: Notes Towards a Conception of Place-Centered Governance." *Competition and Change* 1, no. 1: 31–50.

———. 2000. "Spatialities and Temporalities of the Global: Elements for a Theorization." *Public Culture* 12, no. 1: 215–32.

———. 2006. *Territory, Authority, Rights: From Medieval to Global Assemblages.* Princeton, N.J.: Princeton University Press.

Sasvari, Joanne. 2005. *Paprika: A Spicy Memoir from Hungary.* Toronto: CanWest Books.

SCAHAW 1998. "The Scientific Committee on Animal Health and Animal Welfare (SCAHAW) Opinion on Welfare Aspects for the Production of Foie Gras in Ducks and Geese." http://ec.europa.eu/food/animal/welfare/international/index_en .htm.

Schwartz, Katrina Z. S. 2006. *Nature and National Identity after Communism: Globalizing the Ethnoscape.* Pittsburgh, Pa.: University of Pittsburgh Press.

Shevchenko, Olga. 2009. *Crisis and the Everyday in Postsocialist Moscow.* Bloomington: Indiana University Press.

Shore, Cris. 2000. *Building Europe: The Cultural Politics of European Integration.* New York: Routledge.

Siklosi, P., J. Zoeldi, and E. Singhoffer. 1991. *Alumina Industry, Case Study No. 2.* Report prepared for UNIDO Conference on Ecologically Sustainable Industrial Development, Copenhagen, Denmark, October 14–18.

Spaargaren, Gert, and Arthur P. J. Mol. 1992. "Sociology, Environment, and Modernity: Ecological Modernisation as a Theory of Social Change." *Society and Natural Resources* 5: 323–44.

Spivak, Gayatri. 1988. "Can the Subaltern Speak?" In *Marxism and the Interpretation of Culture*, edited by Cary Nelson and Lawrence Grossberg, 271–313. Urbana: University of Illinois Press.

Staniszkis, Jadwiga. 1992. *The Ontology of Socialism.* Oxford: Clarendon Press.

Stark, David. 1990. "Privatization in Hungary: From Plan to Market or From Plan to Clan?" *East European Politics and Societies* 4, no. 3: 351–92.

———. 1992a. Path Dependence and Privatization Strategies in East Central Europe." *East European Politics and Societies* 6, no. 1: 17–54.

————. 1992b. "The Great Transformation? Social Change in Eastern Europe." *Contemporary Sociology* 21, no. 3: 299–304.

Storz, Cornelia. 2007. "Compliance with International Standards: The EDIFACT and ISO 9000 Standards in Japan." *Social Science Japan Journal* 10: 217–41.

Sun, Andrew. 2009. "Animal Rights Group Targets Restaurant Serving Up Foie Gras Burgers." *South China Morning Post*, April 28: 2.

Swain, Nigel. 1989. "Hungary's Socialist Project in Crisis." *New Left Review* 176: 3–29.

Szempont (Point of View) [Television program]. 2008. No longer available online.

Szirmai, Viktória, and Zsuzsa Lehocki. 1988. *Környezetallapot es érdekviszonyok Ajkan* (State of the environment and relations of interests in Ajka). Manuscript. Budapest: Department of Sociology, the College of Political Science of the Hungarian Socialist Workers' Party.

Taylor, Charles. 1994. "The Politics of Recognition." In *Multiculturalism: Examining the Politics of Recognition*, edited by Charles Taylor and Amy Gutmann, 25–74. Princeton, N.J.: Princeton University Press.

Ticktin, Hillel. 1992a. *Origins of the Crisis in the USSR: Essays on the Political Economy of a Disintegrating System*. Armonk, N.Y.: M. E. Sharpe.

————. 1992b. "Permanent Chaos Without a Market: The Non-Latinamericanization of the USSR." *Studies in Comparative Communism* 25, no. 3: 242–56.

Timmermans, Stefan, and Steven Epstein. 2010. "A World of Standards but not a Standard World: Toward a Sociology of Standards and Standardization." *Annual Review of Sociology* 36: 69–89.

Tóásó, Szilvia. 2006. *Eu-Konform Hízott Libamáj Előállítás Hazai Megoldásának Ökonómiai Kérdései* (The economic issues of producing EU-conforming foie gras domestically). Doctoral thesis. Nyugat-Magyarországi Egyetem Mezőgazdaság- És Élelmiszertudományi Kar, Mosonmagyaróvár, Hungary.

Todorova, Maria. 1997. *Imagining the Balkans*. New York: Oxford University Press.

Trienekens, Jacques, and Peter Zuurbier. 2008. "Quality and Safety Standards in the Food Industry, Developments and Challenges." *International Journal of Production Economics* 113, no. 1: 107–22.

Tsing, Anna. 2000. "The Global Situation." *Cultural Anthropology* 15, no. 3: 327–60.

————. 2005. *Friction: An Ethnography of Global Connections*. Princeton, N.J.: Princeton University Press.

————. 2009. "Supply Chains and the Human Condition." *Rethinking Marxism* 21, no. 2: 148–76.

UNESCO. n.d. "Gastronomic Meal of the French." http://www.unesco.org/culture/ich/index.php?lg=en&pg=00011&RL=00437.

Unnevehr, Laurian J. 2000. *The Economics of HACCP: Costs and Benefits*. St. Paul, Minn.: Eagan Press.

Unnevehr, Laurian, and Nancy Hirschhorn. 2000. *Food Safety Issues in the Developing World*. Washington, D.C.: The World Bank.

Urry, John. 2000. *Sociology Beyond Societies: Mobilities for the Twenty-First Century*. New York: Routledge.

Vedder, Anton, ed. 2007. *NGO Involvement in International Governance and Policy: Sources of Legitimacy*. Leiden, the Netherlands: Martinus Nijhoff.

Venâncio, Armando, and Russell Paterson. 2007. "The Challenge of Mycotoxins." In *Food Safety: A Practical and Case Study Approach,* edited by Anna McElhatton and Richard J. Marshall, 24–49. New York: Springer.

Verdery, Katherine. 1994. "What Was Socialism, and Why Did It Fall?" In *What Was Socialism and What Comes Next?,* 19–38. Princeton, N.J.: Princeton University Press.

———. 1999. "Fuzzy Property: Rights, Power, and Identity in Transylvania's Decollectivization." In *Uncertain Transition: Ethnographies of Change in the Postsocialist World,* edited by Michael Burawoy and Katherine Verdery, 53–82. Lanham, Md.: Rowman & Littlefield.

———. 2004. "The Property Regime of Socialism." *Conservation and Society* 2, no. 1: 191–98.

Vogel, David, and Robert A. Kagan, eds. 2004. *The Dynamics of Regulatory Change: How Globalization Affects National Regulatory Policies.* Berkeley: University of California Press.

Wedel, Janine R. 1998. *Collision and Collusion: The Strange Case of Western Aid to Eastern Europe, 1989–1998.* New York: St. Martin's Press.

Wilk, Richard. 1995. "Learning to be Local in Belize: Global Systems of Common Difference." In *Worlds Apart: Modernity Through the Prism of the Local,* edited by Daniel Miller, 110–33. London: Routledge.

Winner, Langdon. 1986. *The Whale and the Reactor: A Search for Limits in an Age of High Technology.* Chicago: University of Chicago Press.

Wolff, Larry. 1994. *Inventing Eastern Europe: The Map of Civilization on the Mind of the Enlightenment.* Stanford, Calif.: Stanford University Press.

Worster, Donald. 1979. *Dust Bowl: The Southern Plains in the 1930s.* New York: Oxford University Press.

———. 1985. *Rivers of Empire: Water, Aridity and the Growth of the American West.* New York: Pantheon.

Youatt, Rafi. 2011. "Power, Pain, and the Interspecies Politics of Foie Gras." *Political Research Quarterly* 20, no. 10: 1–16.

Young, Iris Marion. 1990. *Justice and the Politics of Difference.* Princeton, N.J.: Princeton University Press.

INDEX

Actor Network Theory (ANT), 115–133
adulteration, 21, 25–27
aflatoxin, 20, 26, 27, 34–40, 99, 105, 125, 139n18
aluminum production, 71–72, 78–80
animal rights, 22, 45–47, 50–59, 61–67, 127, 141n1, 141n5, 142n17, 144n6

Böröcz, József, 38, 96–98, 128, 138n11
Burawoy, Michael, 17, 113, 138n11

certification, 22, 33–34, 44, 100–103, 132–133, 139n10
China, 47, 54–55
civilization, 109–110
COMECON, 3, 139n8
Comaroff, Jean and John. *See* cultural commodification
cultural commodification, 106–107

democracy, 1–2, 7, 11–12, 16, 89–90, 101–111, 119, 121, 125, 131
democratization, 11, 75, 90

ecological modernization, 92, 100
ethics. *See* animal rights; moral sovereignty
European Commission, 33, 86, 94, 128, 144n6
European Union: accession to, 1–40, 60–61, 90, 92, 103, 128, 134–135; Common Agricultural Policy (CAP), 43, 62, 139n12; Eastern Enlargement, 11, 26, 32, 130 (*see also* European Union: accession to); Referendum on membership of, 5–7

farmers, 21–24, 47–49, 52–53, 56, 58–68, 127, 128–131, 139n12, 141n4, 142n16. *See also* European Union: Common Agricultural Policy (CAP)
Fehérkereszt (White Cross), 52–53, 57
fictitious commodity, 131–132. *See also* Polanyi, Karl
FIDESZ (Alliance of Young Democrats), 2–3
figured world, 111, 145n16
foie gras: boycott of, 45–47, 50–61, 64, 67–68, 98, 103, 146n6; production of, 24, 31, 45, 47–50, 64–67. *See also* animal rights
food safety, 25–29, 31–34, 37–44, 54, 100–103, 126–128, 140n32
force-feeding. *See* gavage
Four Paws (FP). *See* foie gras: boycott of
France, 45–47, 54, 56–59, 66–67, 70, 117, 120, 130
Frankfurt School, 133
free trade. *See* trade liberalization
friction, 13–16, 43–44, 75, 91, 118
fuzziness, 12–14

gap, 10; Hetherington's concept of, 88–89; Tsing's concept of, 89–91
gavage, 45–48, 51–57, 59, 65–67, 141n7, 141n8
geographic indicators (GIs), 24, 44, 29–31, 107, 139n16, 140n31, 142n16
global assemblages, 117–118
global ethnography, 15–18
governance, 98, 104, 117, 128
governmentality, 63, 97, 117
Greenpeace, 82, 85

ZSUZSA GILLE is Associate Professor of Sociology at the University of Illinois at Urbana-Champaign. She is author of *From the Cult of Waste to the Trash Heap of History: The Politics of Waste in Socialist and Postsocialist Hungary* (Indiana University Press, 2007), coeditor (with Maria Todorova) of *Post-Communist Nostalgia,* and coauthor (with Michael Burawoy et al.) of *Global Ethnography: Forces, Connections and Imaginations in a Postmodern World.*

CPSIA information can be obtained
at www.ICGtesting.com
Printed in the USA
LVOW13s1540230217
525232LV00011B/118/P